Frog Kissers

Spiritual Warfare Is Not a Fairy Tale

Jennifer Kegin

ISBN 979-8-89309-904-1 (Paperback)
ISBN 979-8-89309-905-8 (Digital)

Covenant Books
11661 Hwy 707
Murrells Inlet, SC 29576
www.covenantbooks.com

Contents

Acknowledgments

I have to thank the Lord Jesus Christ for being my partner in this book—the long hours we spent together, with Him giving me inspiration after inspiration, and the many late nights I stayed up with the Holy Spirit guiding my hands and my heart. Thank You, Father God, for birthing this book. Thank You, Lord, for Your insight and Your love for me, which goes way beyond description.

Also, a thank-you goes out to my husband, who backs me hundred-percent and who is my best supporter on this earth. Without Kevin, I would not have been able to do all I've done, especially writing for God. I am in awe of how God has blessed me with a spiritual leader and an awesome man of God. Thank you, my sweetheart, Kevin.

Also, thanks to my three daughters—Kristy, Lana, and Amie—who are always there for me. You are a true inspiration to me and to everyone around you. Your prayers are my strength.

Introduction

Spiritual Warfare

<u>Spiritual = supernatural, relating to the mind, relating to the spirits</u>

<u>Warfare = conflict, especially when vicious and unrelenting war</u>

As I began this book, after a particular struggle with the enemy, by inspiration of the Holy Spirit, this book on spiritual warfare was birthed. Many believers are going around without their armor on or without the knowledge of the power and authority that we have as believers.

I am in high hopes this book will enlighten and help all who read it to go deeper with God. Because without the facts and truths of the spiritual war (which goes on in the heavenlies), we are truly perishing from the lack of knowledge.

Just Kissing Frogs, as in a fairy tale.

Chapter 1

Sleeping Giants

"Equipping Ourselves with the Armor of God"

Spiritual warfare is so real that the devil tries to distort the truth—tries to get us to believe in *Scooby-Doo* warfare. (It looks real, but in the end, you find out it's really only a human acting like a demon.) If Satan can keep us in the dark about the spiritual realm, he can do as he wills, and believe me, he does! Because he comes to steal, kill, and to destroy.

> *"The thief does not come except to steal,*
> *and to kill, and to destroy." (John 10:10)*

But on the flipside, God brings truth to our life and to the spiritual realm.

God wants us smart to the devil's schemes.

Look with me at Ephesians 2:1–7:

> *"And you he made alive, who were dead*
> *to trespasses and sins, in which you once*
> *walked according to the course of this world,*
> *according to the prince of the power of the*
> *air, the spirit who now works in the sons of*
> *disobedience, among whom also we all once*

> *conducted ourselves in the lusts of the flesh, fulfilling the desires of the flesh and of the mind, and were by nature children of wrath, just as the others. But God, who is rich in mercy, because of His great love with which he loved us, even when we were dead in trespasses, made us alive together with Christ (by grace you have been saved), and raised us up together, and made us sit together in the heavenly places in Christ Jesus, that in the ages to come He might show the exceeding riches of His grace in His kindness toward us in Christ Jesus." (Ephesians 2:1–7)*

> *"Having disarmed principalities and powers, He made a public spectacle of them, triumphing over them in it." (Colossians 2:15)*

If we are "lacking knowledge" of God's Word, we are open to deception from our enemy: Satan. There is no other explanation. There is good, and then there is evil. And deception of the enemy leads to confusion. Look at what God says about confusion:

> *"For where envy and self-seeking exist, confusion and every evil thing are there." (James 3:16)*

> *"For God is not the author of confusion but of peace." (1 Corinthians 14:33)*

So if God doesn't author confusion, guess what? The adversary, Satan, does. I didn't write it, God did!

And because of deceit from Satan, people (believers too) get confused because of the lack of knowledge.

> *"My people are destroyed for lack of knowledge." (Hosea 4:6)*

The thing is, our knowledge is as DEEP as we allow it to be or as SHALLOW as we want it to be.

> *"The heart of the prudent acquires knowledge, and the ear of the wise seeks knowledge." (Proverbs 18:15)*

> *"For the Lord gives wisdom; from His mouth come knowledge and understanding." (Proverbs 2:6)*

You and I can read in abundance about knowledge in God's Word. It's there for us. But we tend to believe in the here and now. The *Scooby-Doo* warfare makes more sense to our fleshly human side. We can touch, smell, and feel things right in front of us. But the spiritual realm goes against our real flesh world, literally.

Choosing to ignore the enemy doesn't make him go away. He is very real. What it does is put us in such a state of denial, then we never engage in the VERY real war of the spiritual realm.

Realm: royal domain, kingdom, the region within which anything occurs, prevails, or dominates

Even the *American Dictionary* states the truth concerning the spiritual realm.

> Spiritual: pertaining to spirit, supernatural or spiritualistic, characterized by or suggesting predominance of the spirit, relating to the mind or intellect

Interesting how both words *spiritual* and *realm* have the words *dominates* and *predominance* in their meaning. Satan will dominate in the spiritual realm as long as you and I are uninformed of the existing warfare in this realm.

The spiritual realm seems like *Star Trek* or *War of the Worlds* to so many people because that's what the world teaches. We become "filled to capacity" of the make-believe, enough that we begin to believe the fairy tales like princesses kissing frogs, witches putting spells on people. See the scenario? We become…*Frog Kissers*! Children are inundated (overwhelmed) with the "make-believe" world, taught to believe it's not real. Then as adults, they have no knowledge of the *real* spiritual world in the heavenlies.

> **"In the beginning God created the heavens and the earth." (Genesis 1:1)**

> **"And I will give you the keys of heaven, and whatever you bind on earth will be bound in heaven, and whatever you loose on earth will be loosed in heaven." (Matthew 16:19)**

And also remember Ephesians 2:1–3?

> **"And you He made alive, who were dead in trespasses and sins, in which you once**

walked according to the course of this world, according to the prince of the power of the air, the spirit who now works in the sons of disobedience, among whom also we all once conducted ourselves in the lusts of the flesh, fulfilling the desires of the flesh and of the mind, and were by nature children of wrath, just as the others."

In verse 3, it states "fulfilling the desires of the flesh and of the mind." This is where most of us react: in the flesh through the mind. Therefore, we are not knowledgeable of the spiritual world.

Look at Ephesians 1:17–18:

"That the God of our Lord Jesus Christ, the Father of glory, may give to you the spirit of wisdom and revelation in the knowledge of Him, the eyes of your understanding being enlightened; that you may know what is the hope of His calling, what are the riches of the glory of His inheritance in the saints."

Then in this same chapter of Ephesians, God tells us in verse 21 that Jesus is far above principality and power and might and dominion. Here's the word *dominion* again. Look at the meaning of this word.

<u>Dominion: the power or right of controlling, rule, lands or domains subject to control</u>

God is longing to show us something here. We have dominion of the air, and we can walk in our God-given authority here on the earth!

We can *discern* both good and evil. We should not be unlearned in the things of God. Look at this scripture in Hebrews:

> *[Spiritual immaturity] "For though by this time you ought to be teachers, you need someone to teach you again the first principles of the oracles of God; and you have come to need milk and not solid food. For everyone who partakes only of milk is unskilled in the word of righteousness, for he is a babe. But solid food belongs to those who are of full age, that is, those who by reason of use have their senses exercised to discern both good and evil." (Hebrews 5:12–14)*

We are to be as "children of God walking in authority," being very keenly aware of our enemy. If we are not aware of evil, then we walk around thinking all is "good" around us, and we never engage in the war that is in this realm.

Unknown to most people, we are fighting in this spiritual war every day of our lives.

> *"And do this, knowing the time, that now it is high time to awake out of sleep." (Romans 13:11)*

Many believers are asleep spiritually. So much so that we never engage in or have the knowledge of the war in the heavens. If there is no spiritual warfare, why would God give us "the whole armor of God" in Ephesians 6? Exactly. It is to stand against our enemy's wiles!

<u>Wiles: to trick, to fool, trap or entice, deceitful, cunning, trickery</u>

> *"Finally, my brethren, be strong in the Lord and in the power of His might. Put on the whole armor of God, that you may be able to stand against the wiles [tricks, traps, deceits] of the devil. For we do not wrestle against flesh and blood, but against principalities, against powers, against the rulers of the darkness of this age, against spiritual hosts of wickedness in the heavenly places. Therefore, take up the whole armor of God, that you may be able to withstand in the evil day, and having done all, to stand. Stand therefore, having girded your waist with truth, having put on the breastplate of righteousness, and having shod your feet with the preparation of the gospel of peace; above all, taking the shield of faith with which you will be able to quench all the fiery darts of the wicked one. And take the helmet of salvation, and the sword of the Spirit, which is the word of God; praying always with all prayer and supplication in the Spirit, being watchful to this end with all perseverance and supplication for all the saints." (Ephesians 6:10–18)*

Putting on God's armor enables us to "stand" against the wiles (tricks) of the devil. In verse 12, it clearly states we "wrestle" against NOT flesh and blood but principalities, rulers of darkness of this age, spiritual hosts (that would be many) of wickedness in heavenly places! These verses explain the *unseen* but very *real* fight we are engaged in. (Unless you are spiritually asleep, that is.)

In verse 13 of Ephesians 6, this verse tells us how we are to fight and withstand this war. And it clearly states we can stand through adversity. (WE WIN!) This chapter goes on to explain in detail how we are to "put on" our armor of God. But many are walking around "naked" (exposed) to the enemy of our souls… without God's Word as our armor. That's why we see defeat and deception so rampant in believers; therefore, defeat is also in our churches.

I'd like to go through our armor of God here because it is vital to "wear" and to "put on" our armor that keeps us standing in this spiritual fight.

1) "Gird" means to encircle or bind, surround, enclose, to prepare for action, to equip as with power or strength.
   <u>We are to surround and enclose our waist with the truth!</u>

2) "Put on" means to place, get into a specific position, to place in charge, to set into action, to force.
   <u>We are to get into our specific position of charge, in action and force, with the breastplate of righteousness!</u>

3) "Shod" means a covering, to protect or arm, an external covering, an object resembling position.
   <u>We are to cover and protect the very ground (our position) we walk by arming ourselves with the gospel of peace!</u>

4) "Shield" means to defend against, to protect, a protective barrier.
   <u>Our shield of faith is our defense, protective barrier against ALL the fiery darts of the wicked one!</u>

5) "Helmet" means forms of protective head covering worn by soldiers.

God has given us "protective head covering" over our minds and states clearly <u>by wearing helmets, we ARE soldiers. (Soldiers are in war.)</u>

6) "Sword" means a weapon having various forms, symbol of military power, war, to engage in combat. The Word of God is our weapon! It comes in various forms (for whatever need we have). Don't go into the spiritual battle without IT!

7) *Prayer* means the practice of praying to God, a petition.

8) *Watchful* means alert, closely observant, wakeful.

9) *Perseverance* means steady persistence in a course of action, especially in spite of obstacles.

<u>We are to practice praying to God in alertness, being wakeful in a steady course</u> of action, <u>especially involving spiritual war and all the obstacles it brings!</u>

Remember a couple pages back, we talked about being "awake?" This is so vital to our prayer life! And by praying, we talk to God. We are in communion with Him through prayer. But spiritually asleep, we are paying no attention to the course of action or the spiritual warfare surrounding us.

<u>Asleep: dormant or inactive state, into the state of death</u>

Could this be why so many believers are living defeated lives? No armor. No prayer life. In a state of being asleep. Falling into a state of spiritual death. In denial of the very apparent war of the heavens, choosing to ignore God's Word, which is His direction to each solider. Believers are continuing in life with no real meaning or direction for their faith.

I don't know how else to get you "stirred" up for this spiritual fight in the heavens except to pray over each of you reading this book. I am believing the Holy Spirit will stir you up. So my prayer over you is as follows:

> God, help us to become aware, alert to the realm of the spirit, which we cannot see but which is very real. Help us to take action and to put on our armor as we go into battle. Help us with our unbelief. And may we become full of knowledge for this very real war! Continue to nudge us, Holy Spirit, and awaken our sleeping souls to the truth! May we put on our equipment as Your soldiers. And in this war realize we do WIN! Amen.

Chapter 2

Preparing for the War

"Learning to Battle with Our Mouth"

Prepare: to put things or oneself in readiness, get ready, to prepare for war

One of the areas we have to prepare for this spiritual war is our mouth.

Look at the meaning of *mouth*.

Mouth: to form with the lips, where flowing water is discharged

"He who believes in Me, as the Scripture has said, out of his heart will flow rivers of living waters." (John 7:38)

River: any abundant stream, outpouring, a natural stream of water of fairly large size flowing in a definite course

As water is a force, the sword (Word of God) is our power, our authority.

Our ability to fight comes from the Word, or sWord.

When we use our (mouth) words in battle, the ability to have powerful flowing rivers of life come forth. As the Scripture states, if you believe in Him, your heart (your mouth) will flow with the strength of a river!

Our mouth will speak as an abundant stream of outpouring in "large size" in a definite course. I must ask, Where are your words going? What course are your lips taking you?

"Fight"—a battle or combat. We are to *fight* with our God-given ability as with a force like a mighty river! If we weren't in a battle, the author, Paul, would have never mentioned the word *fight*. Interestingly, the word *fight* is found 170 times in the Bible!

"Fight the good fight of faith." (1 Timothy 6:12)

I believe so much of the time, as believers, we ignore the hard things that we read in the Word like *fight*, *battle*, or *combat*. We are inclined to focus more on words like *peace*, *love*, and *blessings*. Don't we?

But this book, by inspiration of the Holy Spirit, is about spiritual warfare, our fights and our struggles. It is a book to furnish you with weapons to win our conflict with the enemy: Satan.

In this chapter, I would like to really emphasize and dissect a few different weapons available for combat, for our spiritual fight.

<u>"The Weapons—Our Defense in Combat"</u>

<u>Defensive: protective, resisting attack</u>

Our defensive weapons are the following:

The sWord of God

It is quoted many times in the Bible. "The word of the Lord."

> **"But the word of the Lord endures forever." (1 Peter 1:25)**

> **"So the word of the Lord grew mightily and prevailed." (Acts 19:30)**

> **"And the sword of the Spirit, which is the word of God." (Ephesians 6:17)**

If we are to be defensive against the enemy, protective and resisting attack, we must be equipped with the sWord, the Word of God. We must use the Word of God as our weapon in warfare. In Matthew 4, when Jesus was taken to the wilderness by the devil, He used the Word. Look at verse 10:

> **"Then Jesus said to him, "Away with you, Satan! For it is written, 'You shall worship the Lord your God, and Him only you shall serve.'" (Matthew 4:10)**

Jesus used the Word to fight off the enemy in His struggle and battle in the wilderness. What makes us think it'll be any different for us?

Shield of Faith

> **"Above all, taking the shield of faith with which you will be able to quench all the fiery darts of the wicked one." (Ephesians 6:16)**

> **"Watch, stand fast in the faith, be brave, be strong." (1 Corinthians 16:13)**

> **"I have fought the good fight, I have finished the race, I have kept the faith." (2 Timothy 4:7)**

I have not listed all of our defensive weapons that are in the Holy Bible. There are so many. But we must know that the sWord of the Lord is the most important weapon for our defense. It is our lifeline, and it is given by inspiration of God. It is ours to use if we only will awake from our state of sleep and begin to act as who we are: soldiers of the Most High God! As Timothy states, "Finish the race." Don't quit because the going gets hard. FINISH!

<u>Offensive: characterized by attack, aggressive, the position of attack, an aggressive movement</u>

We will look at two offensive weapons: watchful and alert/prepared

Watchful

> **"And what I say to you, I say to all: "Watch!" (Mark 13:37)**

"Therefore, let us not sleep, as others do, but let us watch and be sober." (1 Thessalonians 5:6)

"Watch and pray, lest you enter into temptation." (Revelations 3:2)

"Be watchful, and strengthen the things which remain." (Matthew 26:41)

Look at the meaning of *watch*: <u>to be alertly on the lookout, to keep awake, remain vigilant as for protection, to keep guard.</u>

The Bible is full of offensive weapons, but I do believe the most important one for us is to stay alert and watch. If Jesus warned us to be awake and to remain watchful, it is for our protection. If we are asleep, we cannot keep guard, and we will miss when the enemy comes in to kill, steal, and destroy.

That is the bottom line. When we spiritually are asleep, we are easy targets for Satan to entrap us. The enemy's intention is to keep us spiritually asleep. He does not want believers to be aware of this war. He wants us to be asleep and unaware of the war in the principalities that are being fought in the air.

So I say to you, "Spiritually watch!"

Alert/Prepared

<u>Alert: fully aware, wide awake, keen, swift, agile, a warning of impending storm</u>

"Be ready in season and out of season." (2 Timothy 4:2)

"Prepare yourself and be ready." (Ezekiel 38:7)

> *"Proclaim this among the nations: Prepare for war! Wake up the mighty men, let all the men of war draw near, let them come up." (Joel 3:9)*

Look again at the meaning of *prepare*: <u>Prepare: **to** put things or oneself in readiness, get ready, to prepare for war.</u>

As we end this chapter, I would like to urge you, if you're not prepared for the spiritual war, get yourself ready. God is calling us, as believers, as soldiers in the spiritual war, to be awake, fully aware of our spiritual surroundings and to fight swiftly and to be agile. He is warning us to be prepared for the war, to be alert and watchful. Don't be asleep when the enemy attacks. Stay spiritually awake!

Our ability to fight comes with God's Word, our sWord. May your mouth take you on a course to fight the good fight of faith!

Chapter 3

The Lineup

"God's Great Army"

Joel 2 is one of my most favorite scriptures in the Bible. It gives me hope and courage to fight this spiritual war. And when I think of "preparing" ourselves for war, it always makes me think of Joel 2.

This chapter in Joel is titled "The Day of the Lord." I encourage you to put this book down, go read Joel 2, then you will understand this chapter more clearly.

As you've read Joel 2, you can clearly see they were preparing for war, sounding alarms for His coming. It describes God's people throughout the chapter. Look at verse 2:

> *"People come, great and strong." (Joel 2:2)*

> *"A fire devours before them. Nothing shall escape them." (Joel 2:3)*

Then in verse 4, he starts to describe believers as men and women in war.

"Their appearance is like the appear-
ance of horses; And like swift steeds, so they
run." (Joel 2:4)

"With a noise like chariots over moun-
taintops they leap, like a noise of a flaming
fire that devours stubble, like a strong people
set in battle array." (Joel 2:5)

Then in verse 6 Joel begins to describe how others see this great army of God.

"Before them the people writhe in pain,
all faces are drained of color." (Joel 2:6)

As God's army, we should be people who are full of power and God's might!

Look how interesting verses 7–9 are:

"They run like mighty men, they climb
the wall like men of war; everyone marches in
formation, and they do not break ranks. They
do not push one another, everyone marches in
his own column; Though they lunge between
the weapons, they are not cut down. They run
to and fro in the city, they run on the wall;
they climb into the houses, they enter at the
windows like a thief." (Joel 2:7–9)

I've got to take a few lines here to pick apart these verses, to explain how the Holy Spirit has revealed these to me. These verses are speaking of God's church, the believers. Sadly, we see many believers who "break" their rank, who push for notoriety, for attention, for control. We see many church leaders who have a hard time staying (let alone marching) in their own "column." Therefore, when we lunge between the weapons (of our warfare we endure), we get cut down. There should be order in every army. God's army much of the time has been out of order—soldiers, sadly, falling at the hands of their own.

If we (the army of God) stay in our God-assigned positions, we will not be "cut down" by the weapons in which the enemy brings. When we are in formation, marching in unison, this is when we truly become His army. Until this takes place, we are like "sitting ducks" of prey for Satan.

As you see in verse 9, we (army of God) can

"run to and fro in the city." (Joel 2:9)

The army of God has access in places of war which seems impossible to the fleshly human mind because this fight takes place in the spiritual realm.

In verse 10 of Joel 2, Joel describes how the earth reacts before God's army:

> ***"The earth quakes before them, the heavens tremble; the sun and moon grow dark, and the stars diminish their brightness." (Joel 2:10)***

Interesting how much authority our army carries that even the earth and the heavens are subject to us! This should get you excited here!

Verse 11 ends this description of God's army in a very profound and powerful way:

> ***"The Lord gives voice before His Army. For His camp is very great. For strong is the One who executes His word. For the day of***

> *the Lord is great and terrible; who can endure it?" (Joel 2:11)*

So to recap verse 11, God goes ahead of us and prepares the way for His army. His army (us, you and I, believers) are awesome through Him. And performing God's Word strengthens us for the war.

Joel goes on in this chapter to tell believers about repentance before God. If we've been one of the army who's pushed or possibly fallen out of rank, God is faithful to forgive. Therefore, we can move forward and get back into formation (our position in the army).

Let me try and illustrate something for you: As a marching band, if you've ever been in a marching band, you'll understand this concept of "marching in formation." One wrong step (march) and the whole band is out of whack. Everyone becomes out of position. I was in a band in high school and remember this well! But it is easy to get right back into rhythm. And it is the same with our God.

"The Unforced Rhythms of Grace"

Look what Jesus says in Matthew 11:28–29 (MSG):

> *"Are you tired? Worn out? Burned out on religion? Come to Me. Get away with Me and you'll recover your life. I'll show you how to take a real rest. Walk with Me and work with Me—watch how I do it. Learn the unforced rhythms of grace." (Matthew 11:28–29)*

<u>Rhythm: movement with uniform, mea-
sured movement</u>

As believers, God is calling us to march in rhythm, measuring every movement and staying in "uniform." Don't get out of your uniform! There is a rank for each one of us in God's great army.

It's time we become concerned about the ranks. They're falling out at extreme numbers! If you rescue a fallen soldier, be sure to put them on your shoulders as you continue to march to God's unforced rhythms of grace.

<u>"Humility in the Army"</u>

"God resists the proud, but gives grace to the humble." (James 4:6)

It's very tempting to get out of step in God's army. We think we know better than God, our Sergeant. We tend to let pride cloud our eyes, and we don't see with humility. It's vitally important to recognize pride in our lives. We each have to deal with prideful flesh! Let God lift you up. That's the place of true leadership: trusting God to lead us, not trying to control by our own efforts.

<u>Grace: favor, mercy, pardon as one of the</u>
elect

"My grace is sufficient for you, for My strength is made perfect in weakness." (2 Corinthians 12:9)

Stay in formation in God's great army! Don't get out of step! Be repentant if you do step out of rank. God's grace is more than sufficient. He always forgives a repentant heart. And we are able to step right back into formation in His army.

Chapter 4

Mind Over Matter

"The Combat Field"

Have you ever had to use your hands to fight? Of course, all of us have in our life at one time or another. Swatting mosquitoes. Pushing open a heavy door. But have you ever "fought" in your mind, pushed around thoughts in your mind?

Look how 1 Peter 4:1 describes our minds:

"Therefore, since Christ suffered for us in the flesh, arm yourselves also with the same mind." (1 Peter 4:1)

And did you notice the word *arm*? This is a warfare scripture; he tells us to "arm" ourselves. Look at the meaning of *arm*:

Arm: a combat branch of the field artillery, power, might, strength, authority

So when Peter tells us to arm ourselves with the same mind as Christ, he is saying, "Empower yourself with Christ's mind in might, strength, and God-given authority; go into combat equipped with heavenly thoughts and not with our flesh carnal minds."

The spiritual war is in our minds. Did you hear what I just said? "The spiritual war is in our minds!" If the war was physical, if we were able to touch it with our hands, we'd GET it. But since it's spiritual, we struggle with the unseen wiles of the enemy.

We can't see the war, but it's definitely real. We can't touch it with our physical hands; that's why so many believers struggle to stay in the safe confines of God's protection. Getting outside of His will always causes us to struggle.

> *"And do not be conformed to this world, but be transformed by the renewing of your mind." (Romans 12:2)*

The mind! What a hard thing to get under control! The intellect! The thoughts! The arguments in our own heads!

"<u>Mind of Christ</u>"

But there IS hope. We can put on, arm ourselves, and combat with the mind of Christ!

> *"And be renewed in the Spirit of your mind." (1 Corinthians 2:16)*

> *"But we have the mind of Christ." (Ephesians 4:23)*

> *"Set your mind on things above, not things on the earth." (Colossians 3:2)*

"Gird up the loins of your mind." (1 Peter 1:13)

You're probably asking, Why can't I "transform" and "renew" my mind that runs in wild, unlovely places? (Glad you asked!)

My answer: Because we don't arm, put on or gird our minds with the Word of God!

Again, I want to remind you what *gird* means.

Gird: surround, enclose

So we must surround and enclose our minds with the Word!

Then because we do not combat against spiritual forces with our spirit, we try and war against the spiritual with our carnal minds. AND then we wonder why we're in a fix! It's how we conduct our minds, our thoughts. Do we guide/escort our minds into godly areas, or are we taking it to fleshly areas?

Let's take the time here to break it down. Let's look at our minds first.

MIND = FLESH

Without the help of God's Word, cleansing and renewing our flesh/mind, we are carnal. We are facing our enemy in a naked state, wide open to the wiles of and the snares of Satan.

Let me explain it this way: You are defeated and overcome when you fight (combat, war) with only your flesh-mind.

Now, on the other hand, in the spiritual realm, as we war with God's Word, providing us with His wisdom and His strength, we are fighting with authority. Destined to win!

"A Believer's Authority"

Now let's look at our spiritual authority which is what we should be fighting our spiritual war with. God's Word shows us exactly what our authority is.

> *"Whatever things you ask in prayer, believing, you will receive." (Matthew 21:22)*

> *"Speak these things, exhort, and rebuke with all authority. Let no one despise you." (Titus 2:15)*

> *"I charge you therefore before God and the Lord Jesus Christ." (2 Timothy 4:1)*

> <u>Charge</u>: to impute, to instruct authoritatively, to fill with the quantity, an <u>impetuous attack as of soldiers</u>

I charge you with authoritative instructions to fill yourself with quantity and power, to attack with great force (impetuously) as the soldiers of God's great army!

Look at Matthew 11:12:

> *"And the violent take it by force."* *(Matthew 11:12)*

Have you ever taken anything spiritually by force? Maybe salvation over a family member or a friend? Maybe you prayed without relent until you saw your prayer answered? You were forceful, not giving up.

In this same forceful manner, the mind can be transformed by renewing it to the will of God. We struggle with our minds because we have never "subdued" it to God's Word.

Quoting scripture over our mind is a good start. Let your mind know you mean business—that you will win this battle, that you are more than a conqueror!

> *"In all these things we are more than conquerors through Him who loved us."*
> *(Romans 8:37)*

When we win the battle over our minds, we win in every area of our thought life, which then equips us to win/take authority over ALL other areas of the flesh.

Arm yourself for this battle, or you will war in a wide-open naked state of defeat! BUT when we are armed with the Word,

> *"the peace of God, which surpasses all understanding, will guard your hearts and minds through Christ Jesus." (Philippians 4:7)*

I want my heart and my mind to be guarded by God's peace! Don't you?

Chapter 5

Distinguishing Your Enemy

"Know the Enemy's Tactics"

Deceived: to mislead by a false appearance, falsely persuade others

Each one of us has been deceived or misled falsely or even persuaded by others. In the same manner, our adversary (Satan) tries to deceive and mislead believers.

"Do not be deceived my beloved brethren." (James 1:16)

"And Jesus answered and said to them: "Take heed that no one deceives you." (Matthew 24:4)

"The devil, who deceived them." (Revelations 20:10)

I think we all can truthfully say we know who the deceiver is: he is our enemy, Satan. The Word shows us over and over to be aware and not let him deceive us. Yet there are deceptions among believers in the here and now, not just in the Bible.

Warnings should not be taken lightly, and especially not straight from the mouth of Jesus Himself! We cannot ignore the danger of impending evil and the urgency of Jesus's words.

If I stood up, blew a trumpet, would you listen? Yes. It's an alarm—a loud noise that would get your attention. You would look to see what was going on and, more than likely, you would take heed to what was happening. This is how Jesus wants us to react to His Word. Listening. Really hearing with response to His advice. Let's direct our attention upon the meaning of *listen*:

<u>Listen: attend closely for the purpose of</u> <u>hearing, heed, obey, to give ear to, hear</u>

"Now therefore, listen to me, my children; pay attention to the words of My mouth." [Capitalization is mine.] (Proverbs 7:24)

There are purposes to listening carefully and extremely attentive. God doesn't want us to be unaware of our enemy! God especially wants us to be aware of Satan's deceptions.

"For the Lord gives wisdom; From His mouth come knowledge and understanding." (Proverbs 2:6)

"Be sober, be vigilant; because your adversary the devil walks about like a roaring lion, seeking whom he may devour." (1 Peter 5:8)

Know, understand, be aware of, pay close attention to, and acquire knowledge of the enemy who will deceive even the elect.

<u>The spiritual accomplishments you make here on the earth will be determined by how you view the enemy.</u>

You may ask, Is Satan really a threat? Should we just ignore his existence?

And I answer you: Yes, he is! And no, we cannot ignore him. Look at what even Jesus had to go through in Matthew 4:

> *"Then Jesus was led up by the Spirit into the wilderness to be tempted by the devil. And when He had fasted forty days and forty nights, afterward He was hungry." (Matthew 4:1–2)*

> *"Now when the tempter came to Him." (Verse 3)*

> *"Then the devil took Him up into the holy city, set Him on the pinnacle of the temple." (Verse 5)*

> *"Again, the devil took Him up on an exceedingly high mountain, and showed Him all the kingdoms of the world and their glory. And he said to Him "All these things I will give You if You will fall down and worship me." (Verses 8–9)*

> *"Then the devil left Him, and behold, angels came and ministered to Him." (Verse 11)*

Read Matthew 4 and you will get a better idea of how Jesus was under a very real spiritual war and how He was onslaught by evil. What makes you think it'll be any different for you and I?

Especially if we are standing up for godly principles and testifying of our Lord and Savior.

Just as Jesus did in Matthew 4.

> *"But He answered and said, "It is written." (Matthew 4:4)*

> *"Jesus said to him, "It is written again." (Verse 7)*

> *"Then Jesus said to him, "Away with you, Satan! For it is written." (Verse 10)*

We are obligated to use God's Word in life's situations of ups and downs. There is a very real need to arm ourselves with the Word of God (our sWord, Ephesians 6). It is our protection, our defense against Satan.

If I went into a boxing match without my boxing gloves, I'd lose. It's the same for our spiritual match with the devil; if we go into battle without our sWords, we lose.

Knowing my enemy, Satan, is out to kill, steal, and to destroy me, it is essential (life or death spiritually) for me to carry my sWord every minute of every day.

NOT carrying my weapon of war, I become a victim of the enemy.

> <u>Victim: a person who is deceived by his</u> <u>own ignorance</u>

And hopefully this book influences you to obtain all the knowledge available so you can be aware and ready to combat Satan.

Don't ignore the danger of his tactics!

<u>Tactics: any mode of procedure for gaining advantage or success</u>

Satan will go to all lengths to take advantage of you. He will die trying to succeed. Literally. Satan is destined for hell, and he's aware of his future. He hates God, and he hates His creation—you and I.

"Do not marvel, my brethren, if the world hates you." (1 John 3:13)

We have to focus on the truth of God's Word and equip ourselves with the sWord to fight against our enemy.

If you know your enemy, then you will know his ways, his devices, then you will know how to react in the face of adversity. Satan loses. We win. That's a promise!

Father God, help us to not be deceived and to be carriers of Your truth! May we have knowledge of our enemy's tactics. Give us the necessary ammo to not be a victim of Satan! May we always carry our sWords and win the battle! Amen.

Chapter 6

The Narrow Road

<u>"Living in a Harsh World"</u>

But Jennifer, you ask, How can I cope with the enemy's tactics? How do I stay above and not beneath? Can I conquer in the midst of all this evil?

Glad you asked!

Yes, you can. You "cope" with God's Word. Stay in formation in the great army and don't get out of rank. Yes, you can conquer.

<u>Conqueror: to overcome by force, win in war, to gain a victory over, overcome</u>

I want to talk about Noah here. Just think about the story of Noah (Genesis chapters 5–9). God asked him to build a boat, no rain in the forecast (not for a long time). But under extreme pressure, Noah built the ark. He was five hundred years old when he started and six hundred years old when he actually got in the ark! One hundred years of building the ark. Then he and his family, and all the animals, lived in the ark for 370 days; that's over a year! (And I get impatient waiting only one day for something!)

How Noah must've felt is beyond our knowledge really. But one thing is certain: Noah was a conqueror! He didn't give up. He heard God's plan, and he accomplished that plan. God forgives me for ever complaining, and I'm not even sixty-five years old!

What if Noah would've given up, gotten off God's plan, gotten out of formation, and not built the ark? Now, that's a thought. But we can sure learn from Noah's steadfast spirit. Because if you're like me, we whine when we don't "get" the smallest of things!

<u>"The Narrow Way"</u>

The Bible talks about the narrow road in Matthew 7.

> *"Because narrow is the gate, and difficult is the way which leads to life, and there are few who find it." (Matthew 7:14)*

Endurance is the key that unlocks our strength to continue the duration of our spiritual life on earth. We have the ability to finish strong too, just as Noah did. It's called FAITH—maintaining our lives with God through faith.

> <u>Endurance: the ability or strength to continue, lasting quality, duration</u>

> *"But you, beloved, building yourselves up on your most holy faith, praying in the Holy Spirit, keep yourselves in the love of God, looking for the mercy of our Lord Jesus Christ unto eternal life." (Jude 1:20–21)*

Faith will build us up and strengthen our life in Him. We can never quit; we must strive for a life of faith right up to our death. Then we have eternal life with God to look forward to!

There's action on our part to live as God has planned for us to in lasting quality strength right up to the end. The action words we see in Jude 1:20–21 are the following:

- *Building.* To mold, form, or create; the act or practice of constructing; to establish, increase, or strengthen.
- *Praying.* Praise, thanks, to bring, to make petition for, to enter into a spiritual communion with God.
- *Keeping.* Agreement, to hold or retain in one's possession, to maintain control of, to continue in a given position, course, or action.
- *Looking.* To use one's sight in seeking, searching, examining, watching; to face or front; to see; search for; to anticipate; expect.

Practice establishing your strength by having a relationship with God, maintaining control of and searching for it. Watch for God to see you through life's hardest battles. He does see us through. He always has, and He always will.

> *"Fear not, for I am with you; Be not dismayed, for I am your God, I will strengthen you. Yes, I will help you, I will uphold you with My righteous right hand." (Isaiah 41:10)*

Like Noah, we endure to the end. It takes action on our part and determination to finish the race as a conqueror. We have the best weapon; it's our sWord—the Word of our God.

Before we go on, I want to look at one aspect of how God's Word works for us. There are so many scriptures that give us strength and knowledge. Look at Jeremiah 23:29:

"Is not My word like a fire?" says the Lord, "And like a hammer that breaks the rock in pieces?" (Jeremiah 23:29)

Fire: brilliance, strength, to set on fire, to inspire, be kindled, eager, ardent, zealous
Hammer: to beat or drive, to fasten, to assemble, to shape, to form, construct, to produce by force, state strongly, aggressively, and effectively, emphasize by repetition

This tells us that our Word is our strength to set a fire in us, inspires us to not give up, kindles us with a zealous and eager desire to live for God!

We can never give up the fight! We've got to endure the same as Noah endured. Noah could see the finish line. We must look to the finish line.

Our sWord also is our drive to fasten, assemble, shape, and to form us. To produce by force God's will on the earth. To state strongly and aggressively God's Word, and to see IT be effective in our lives as well as in others. It is like a hammer; we need to emphasize with repetition, not giving up, never quitting. Hitting the mark (the target) with God's Word.

Never give up when the fight gets hard! Be so full of enduring faith and have a tenacity as fire and the Word in you as a hammer hitting the target—as we live for God.

We can cope through anything as long as we practice establishing our faith in God!

An established enduring lifestyle will bring you established faith in God.

Chapter 7

Choosing God's Thoughts

"Deceptions and Being Aware of Who to Blame"

"The heart is deceitful above all things."
(Jeremiah 17:9)

There is a very real deception among believers that Satan is <u>not</u> out to kill, steal, and destroy. I believe this chapter, by inspiration of the Holy Spirit, will bring real knowledge to this ploy of Satan. To begin this chapter, we'll look at deception, where it comes from, and how to battle it effectively.

First, let's take a look at the word *deception*.

<u>Deception: the act of deceiving, something that deceives, fraud</u>

God tells us in James 1:16,

"Do not be deceived, my beloved brethren." (James 1:16)

So God is wanting us to be aware there is going to be deceptions. Jesus even said,

"Take heed that no one deceives you."
(Matthew 24:4)

Sometimes, deception can even be in our own minds. We truly are our own worst enemies much of the time.

> **"If we say we have no sin, we deceive ourselves, and the truth is not in us." (1 John 3:7)**

> **"Let no one deceive himself." (1 Corinthians 3:18)**

Each one of us has been deceived by our own "thoughts." We'd like to blame the devil for our actions: "The devil made me do it." But in reality, we know we are the only one to blame for our actions. Deception can be subtle and pretty sly. Our enemy will prey on us at times of weakness. He will forever prey upon us until we go to be with our Lord in heaven.

But it's vitally important to recognize where our thoughts are taking us. Because a thought will be carried out eventually if we spend much time on thinking upon it.

What are you thinking upon? I can deceive my own mind into thinking I am of no value in the kingdom of God, or I can think on things above. I choose. You choose.

> **"Seek those things which are above....**
> **Set your mind on things above, not on things**
> **on the earth." (Colossians 3:1–2)**

When our minds are "set" on the Lord and we are "seeking" Him, then we will walk in knowledge and not deception. And I'll remind you here again: you need to know the Word, our sWord. We have to fight deceiving thoughts with our sWord and not our flesh.

Let's talk about choices. You are choosing to sit down and read this book, right? No one made you do it. But it first became a thought, *That book looks like it might help me out*. Then you end up picking it up and reading it. Choices.

How many wrong choices have I made in my life? Too numerous to count!

But God is faithful to forgive. His mercies are new every morning!

"Through the Lord's mercies we are not consumed, because His compassions fail not. They are new every morning; Great is Your faithfulness." (Lamentations 3:22–23)

"Choose for yourselves this day whom you will serve." (Joshua 24:15)

We will be faced each and every day with choices. And I am a firm believer that everything we do is spiritual. There are no maybes in serving God! We choose to serve and follow Him, or we choose to turn away from His plan for our life. I choose to sit up at midnight to write this book. You choose to read this book.

<u>Choose: the power or opportunity to choose, carefully selected</u>

We need to carefully, prayerfully, select and choose our actions and our words based upon God's Word. Because if we don't, our minds are highly likely going to "steer" us in the opposite direction of God's Word. Have you ever heard the saying, "Your mind can play tricks on you?" It's a very true statement!

I went through a personal time in my life of hardship. In one particular season in our lives, in my marriage to Kevin, we ran from God's plan and ended up almost divorced, and it was hell on earth. Let me tell you! I chose during this time to be angry. Really bitter. Satan deceived me into thinking I had a right to be angry.

But as a child of God, I do not have that right (no matter what). My body is the temple where God resides.

> ***"Do you not know that you are the temple of God and that the Spirit of God dwells in you?" (1 Corinthians 3:16)***

> ***"Do not let the sun go down on your wrath." (Ephesians 4:26)***

> <u>Wrath: fierce anger, deeply resentful indignation</u>

I do believe each person reading this book either has anger or has had anger in their heart. It's not an easy emotion to control. But we must remember to put God's Word, as a shield, around our hearts to protect against anger building up inside and blocking our spiritual reactions.

Anger is just one deception we'll deal with. There are so many deceptions to be aware of. There are many choices to make to be able to keep deceptions at bay. But the very first choice is to choose righteous thoughts and to war against the deceiver of our souls.

> ***"Commit your works to the Lord, and your thoughts will be established." (Proverbs 16:3)***

> ***"For though we walk in the flesh, we do not war according to the flesh. For the weapons of our warfare are not carnal but mighty in God for pulling down strongholds, casting down arguments and every high thing that exalts itself against the knowledge of God,***

> *bringing every thought into captivity to the*
> *obedience of Christ." (1 Corinthians 10:3–5)*

Fighting the battle is our first order of business. We must arm and equip ourselves to go into battle. We must be aware of the battle and have knowledge to be able to come out on top, not beneath.

> *"And the Lord will make you the head*
> *and not the tail; you shall be above only, and*
> *not be beneath, if you heed the commands of*
> *the Lord your God." (Deuteronomy 28:13)*

God fully intends for us to win. If it were not so, He wouldn't have given us His Son. Jesus gives us all authority here on earth.

> *"Behold, I give you the authority to*
> *trample on serpents and scorpions, and over*
> *all the power of the enemy, and nothing shall*
> *by any means hurt you." (Luke 10:19)*

Authority: the power to determine, a power or right delegated or given, the right to control

You, as believers, have the God-given right to control every situation you face!

What authority, delegated rights, and power given to you are you currently using as your weapons to win?

THE CHOICE IS UP TO YOU!

Chapter 8

The Different Angles of Deception

"Arming Ourselves with the Mind of Christ"

To explain deception, I'd like to tell you what happened to me: We moved into a new home. And I don't dream or remember them very often. But just recently, I've had two dreams concerning grandchildren. Fear gripped me after these dreams. I didn't allow my mind to dwell on them very long though. AND...the next day, I had "thoughts" of someone I love killing themselves, just out of the blue. I've never had these thoughts about this loved one before.

To say the least, this made me stop and really examine what was happening. I got my Bible (my sWord), and I sat down, asking the Holy Spirit to give me wisdom and to saturate my mind with His sWord. And this is when I began to "see" what was happening, and I got this revelation:

First, I took authority in Jesus's name over any foul spirits in my new home. Applying the blood of Jesus over everything. (The couple we bought the home from had a son who committed suicide.)

Secondly, I got revelation that the enemy was trying to deceive me and trying to place fear on me.

<u>Fear: a distressing emotion aroused by impending danger whether the threat is real or imagined</u>

The enemy will come at you with many different angles. He's not messing around. He will kill, steal, and he will destroy you at any cost if you are not aware of his tricks and schemes.

Let's talk about dreams first. I try to remember at night to pray over my mind and my dreams before I go to sleep. I do not want to be attacked in the area of dreams. I also watch closely what I allow my eyes and my heart to take in: movies, horror shows, etc. What goes into my heart will eventually come out.

> *"But those things which proceed out of the mouth come from the heart, and they defile a man." (Matthew 15:18)*

Even though I am a believer, I can open doors and allow my flesh to "see" and "hear" opposite of what God wants me to see and to hear. Therefore, I can allow fear to enter my soul, and my soul will dream about that fear.

WA-LA…fear over my grandchildren and someone I love committing suicide.

If the enemy can keep me all bundled up in fears, I am "bound," unable to walk in my God-given authority. In fear, I am worrying (self-imposed) more than I am "warring" against the enemy. See?

Romans 8 explains it pretty clear:

> *"For those who live according to the flesh set the minds on the things of the flesh, but*

> **those who live according to the Spirit, the things of the Spirit." (Romans 8:5)**

The Word of God is really absolute, straightforward, and to the point. We can choose to live for ourselves, or we can choose to live for Him. And there is no in between. That's another deception from the enemy! (But we won't go there right now).

So dreams filled with fear are our flesh minds. But we do have authority through Jesus's blood to dream spiritual dreams. You'll know the difference because God does not give us fear, only the enemy uses scare tactics.

While I'm not an expert on dreams, by all means, I know someone who is. Ask God; He'll be glad to talk with you on the subject, and He'll give you revelation too.

Next, I'd like to cover the deception of "thoughts." We really do allow the enemy to pile crap on us to the point we are believing what we think. Ouch.

A lot of times, I'll "force" my mind and tell it, "You will think on the things above, not the things here on this earth." Because the mind can run one thousand miles a minute and take you into areas that seem okay when in reality it can steal the quality of your spiritual walk with God.

I can't count the numerous times I've stopped doing God's will because my thoughts simply persuaded me to do so. Thoughts like, *God didn't really say that*, or *Is God real?* These are carnal thoughts!

> **"The carnal mind is enmity against God." (Romans 8:7)**

We either think like God or we don't. We either live for Him or we don't. Don't let the enemy deceive you into thinking it's okay to live for yourself. It's actually choosing death. No question about it!

Have you ever just had your mind wander so far off that it was hard to get back to reality? Yes. All of us have, maybe on a daily basis even. Let me give you some weapons to ward off this tactic from the devil.

You can renew your mind! Look at God's Word:

> ***"That you put off, concerning your former conduct, the old man which grows corrupt according to the deceitful lusts, and be renewed in the spirit of your mind, and that you put on the new man which was created according to God, in true righteousness and holiness." (Ephesians 4:22–24)***

This gives me such hope! I can renew my mind. I do have to "put off" the old man with its deceitful lusts and "put on" the new man. This is how God created us to be, in true righteousness and holiness.

Look again at the scripture from 1 Peter 4:1:

> ***"Arm yourselves also with the same mind." (1 Peter 4:1)***

I can arm myself with the mind of Christ! And you betcha, I'm going to! Look at the meaning of *arm* again:

Arm: power, might, strength, authority

So look at this same scripture with the meaning of *arm* placed in it:

> Empower yourself, give yourself might, by putting on strength and authority with the mind of Christ Jesus.

God wants you and I to have minds so impregnated with His Word that we never allow the enemy to steal our God-given rights and authority again.

I've struggled to write this book. It's not a fleshly struggle; it's a spiritual war. The enemy does not want revelation to get into the hands of believers. If the enemy can keep you bound in your fleshly mind, you aren't much of a threat to him. But walking in revelation arms us with power and authority over his tactics.

I pray each one reading this book gets exactly the revelation that you are needing. Because if you're warring against the enemy, you're certainly doing something right. (I think I'm onto something! Will you join me in this fight?)

Arm yourselves! Become a conqueror!

In the next chapter, we'll learn more about becoming a conqueror with God-given authority.

Chapter 9

The Conqueror Subduing

"Walking in Greater Authority on the Earth"

Overcomer: to get the better of a struggle
or conflict, conquer, defeat, to overpower, win

To walk as an overcomer, we must discipline ourselves in obedience to God. That obedience sets us in line to be able to subdue circumstances over our life and also over others' lives as well.

*"But I discipline my body and bring it
into subjection." (1 Corinthians 9:27)*

Subdue: to conquer, bring into subjection,
to overcome, to overpower by superior force

We know Jesus has authority over all things. But let me point out to you what authority YOU have.

*"Most assuredly, I say to you, he who
believes in Me, the works that I do he [that's
us] will do also; and greater works than these
will he [that's us again] do, because I go to
My Father." (John 14:12)*

I believe that REVELATION MOMENTS ARE HAPPENING! Like a light bulb coming on in a dark room!

"You have authority greater than Jesus!"

God gave men dominion at the very beginning of time in Genesis 1:28:

> ***"Be fruitful and multiply; fill the earth***
> ***and subdue [conquer, overcome, overpower]***
> ***it; have dominion over...every living thing***
> ***that moves on the earth." (Genesis 1:28)***

God said it, not Jennifer! God gives us authority. But sadly, many of us believers never get a revelation of just how much power we can walk in! God desires us to be so knowledgeable that we are conquering, subduing, overcoming, and overpowering all things that move, that breathe, or have being.

<u>All: the whole of, the greatest possible,</u>
<u>every, all kinds, everything, entirely, completely</u>

The meaning of ALL is very self-explanatory. We can subdue completely in our sphere of influence—the earth.

<u>"Walls Come Down"</u>

The Bible has many stories of subduing the enemy. But the one that comes to mind is the walls of Jericho coming down in Joshua 6. The army of Joshua, at the orders of God, marched around the walls; in faith, they believed. And God brought the walls down flat. They subdued (conquered) the city. I think the thing to remember here is, we are God's army too. God has provided us a way to win the battle.

Conquering a battle first begins in our intellect, our minds. If I'm a winner, I must think as a winner. But my "thinking" has to be transformed by the Word.

I know I've quoted this scripture in another chapter, but it really warrants being repeated here.

> ***"But be transformed by the renewing of the mind." (Romans 12:2)***

<u>Transformed: to change in condition, convert</u>

We've probably all seen a *Transformer* movie, right? Where the cars transform on our TV screens into a machine ready for combat. Well, in the spiritual realm, this is how we transform our minds, and convert our minds into God's army, by changing our thoughts—just how the *Transformers* transform; we must convert our minds by the Word of God. We may "look" like just a human, but we are "conquerors" underneath the flesh!

<u>"Know Who You Are in God"</u>

It is of utmost importance to know where you stand with God. His Word is Him speaking into your heart and into your spirit man.

> ***"All Scripture is given by inspiration of God, and is profitable for doctrine, for reproof, for correction, for instruction in righteousness, that the man of God may be complete, thor-***

oughly equipped for every good work." (2 Timothy 3:16–17)

God can transform, conform, and rearrange what's not in working order!

He gives us the necessary aide to combat in this war.

Now that the Holy Spirit has given us revelation of our subduing authority here on the earth, let's look at another authority we have.

These are Jesus's words to believers:

"Go therefore and make disciples of all the nations, baptizing them in the name of the Father and of the Son and of the Holy Spirit, teaching them to observe all things that I have commanded you; and lo, I am with you always, even to the end of the age." (Matthew 28:19–20)

"Teaching them to observe all things" sounds like, to me, Jesus wants us to tell others the revelation we've received from Him.

"Freely you have received, freely give." (Matthew 10:8B)

Go: to move or proceed, to reach, to develop, progress

We are called to "GO," reach, and develop God's love in the world and bring His good news to people on the earth. We aren't to only subdue in our own little corner, but we subdue and conquer the enemy for others' benefit also.

If we walk in our authority here on this earth, ALL things are in subjection to us, and we will do greater works than Jesus.

You are a subduing conqueror! It's your right in Jesus's name!

Chapter 10

Deceiving Pride

"The Revelation of God's Unfailing Love"

I touched a small amount on the deception of thinking we don't have to live 100 percent for God. That we're okay just being a believer. I call that *fireproof* thinking. It may sound like this: "I'm going to heaven. God doesn't need me to do anything here on earth. He's God, by all means." or "I'll have fun. I won't give up my sinful lifestyle. God will forgive me."

The enemy will deceive us into thinking it's okay to live whatever way we want. But what we need to realize is that if you're not living for God, you're living for the devil! Ouch!

People tend to think there's always tomorrow when today is the most important day of your life. God told me one time in a complicated season of my life: "Every moment is a God moment." Wow. That made me stop and analyze, *Why do I think it's all about me?*

Look at what Jesus says about riding the fence on living for God:

> *"So then, because you are lukewarm, and neither cold nor hot, I will vomit you out of My mouth." (Revelations 3:16)*

51

"I know you inside and out, and find little to My liking. You're not cold, you're not hot—far better to be either cold or hot! You're stale. You're stagnant. You make Me want to vomit. You brag…I need nothing from anyone." (Revelations 3:16 MSG)

<u>Stale</u>: not fresh, having lost vigor, intelligence, or the like
<u>Stagnant</u>: lack of advancement, inactive, sluggish

May God help us to never be stale or stagnant when it comes to living for Him! I always want to be a sweet aroma to my Jesus!

"For we are to God the fragrance of Christ." (2 Corinthians 2:15)

There are many believers being deceived because the enemy knows how much God loves each of His children.

"But the very hairs of your head are all numbered. Do not fear therefore; you are of more value than many sparrows." (Luke 12:7)

We can't grasp how high or how wide God's love is.

"In this is love, not that we loved God, but that He loved us and sent His Son to be the propitiation for our sins." (1 John 4:10)

"This is the kind of love we are talking about—not that we once upon a time loved

***God, but that He loved us and sent His Son
as a sacrifice to clear away our sins and the
damage they've done to our relationship with
God." (1 John 4:10 MSG)***

I hadn't planned on writing about God's love. But the opposite of the enemy's deception and lies is God's love.

The very answer to the questions, the unanswered problems in our life, is God's love. He loves us with an eternal love, and we choose to live how we feel—fun, sin-filled lives, turning our backs on *true love*.

The world seeks love in all the wrong places when it's right under their noses. Readily available. God's arms are always open to us.

But the deception of the enemy lures them into its deadly grasp—leading to death, hurt, pain, heartaches. And here I think of how Satan fell from heaven (Isaiah 14:12). And sadly, how many people are falling right along beside him.

The deception of pride comes into play. Too proud to live for God. Too proud to give up things or riches. Too proud to kneel before God in humility.

***"Pride goes before destruction, and a
haughty spirit before a fall." (Proverbs 16:18)***

<u>Pride: a high opinion of one's own importance, a becoming sense of what is due to oneself</u>

Our pride separates us from a relationship with God. No ifs, ands, or buts. We can't think of ourselves as being higher than God, or we will fall in our pride, flat on our face.

You are either living for God, or you are living for Satan. Don't allow the enemy to deceive you in thinking otherwise. You are setting yourself up for a hard fall. If it weren't for God's love, we would all be destined for hell.

Not one of us is good enough for heaven without Jesus's death on the cross. He paid the price for our eternal life in heaven. Why is it so hard to live for Him 100 percent with everything we've got?

Because there is deception from the enemy. There is a father of lies lying to you. If you're still questioning this God-life, please ask God to show you what's real and what's a deception. God will answer you. Be ready to hear His answer. Revelation can be shocking! But revelation will also keep you from being deceived in that particular area again.

God loves you so much; He wants you to be aware of your enemy. When we're aware of danger, then we can prepare to combat against the danger. It's not any different with our spiritual enemy. Being aware of the enemy's wiles and tactics can save you from harm and pain and keep you tuned into God's ways.

> **"For to be carnally minded is death, but
> to be spiritually minded is life and peace."
> (Romans 8:6)**

I'll never say it's easy living for God. It's rough. But there's a perfect peace that comes even in the storms of life. Waves beat at the side of the boat, threaten to capsize it, but I put down the anchor and rise above the storm. I face the winds, the hail, and the pouring rain because I can see the finish mark: heaven is my real home. Now that's perfect peace.

> **"You will keep him in perfect peace,
> whose mind is stayed on You, because he
> trusts in You." (Isaiah 26:3)**

If it's perfect peace you're looking for, live for God. You'll find it no matter what you may see surrounding your life.

AND…how could you turn that down?

May God reveal Himself to you as you read this book because He is the only peace you'll ever know. Don't run from the Anchor of your soul. Let Him encompass your heart and still your mind. He's a God of love.

> *"This hope we have as an anchor of the soul, both sure and steadfast." (Hebrews 6:19)*

Chapter 11

Angels of War

"Do You Smell Like Fire?"

"The angel of the Lord encamps all around those who fear Him and delivers him."
(Psalm 34:7)

The role/position of angels in our lives is a role we often have no knowledge of. But if we talk about warfare, then we must talk about the angels who go into war on our behalf—the angels who prepare the way before us, who are guarding over each believer.

If we could physically see into the spiritual realm, we'd be able to see a host of angels as the Word tells us.

"For He shall give His angels charge over you, to keep you in all your ways." (Psalm 91:11)

How do we know angels are angels of war? In 1 Chronicles 21, God sent an angel to destroy Jerusalem. It clearly pictures an angel with a sword. There are only two reasons an angel would carry a sword: to either kill or to defend. In this instance, it was to destroy the people in Jerusalem.

Also, look at Daniel in the lion's den. This is a perfect story of how angels defend us. The angels were sent by God to shut the lions' mouths.

If we read the book of Revelation, there are numerous accounts of angels sent by God to either destroy or defend.

I've had a few visions of angels. Although it's hard to explain the exactness of these visions, I think I will try to paint you a picture of the angels I've seen.

We were on a mission trip in Romania. During church services, I've seen angels all around the balcony above us. Each angel had ancient armor on—old helmets like Roman soldiers would've worn. I didn't see faces, only gray images, but I knew very distinctly that I was witnessing a vision of angels.

On the flipside, I also have seen evil fallen angels, demons, also in Romania. I had a vision of these demons trying to get to our group of missionaries. They had cloaks on with hoods that hid their faces. But I knew beyond any doubt they were demons. There was a circle of them looking down on our group, but they were unable to reach or harm us because we had a hedge of protection over us, the blood of Jesus covering us.

Also, I've seen angels with wings who have kept my children from harm.

Even my eight-year-old granddaughter, Mercy, has seen many angels, protecting her and our family.

I think God longs for believers to get the revelation of angels who are assigned to each of us and also the assignment from God over our lives for protection from these angels.

Another time, I had a vision of a very large angel hovering over our church during praise and worship. Just watching us. Now, why else would an angel be watching God's people except for protection? There is no other explanation.

I'd like to look at the Word of God and gather information here that tells us about angels:

- Angels praise God (Psalm 148:2)
- They strengthened Jesus (Luke 22:43)
- They talk to men (Zechariah 2:3)
- They are ministers for God (Hebrews 1:7)
- They are flames of fire (Hebrews 1:7)
- They fight for God and for us (Revelation 12:7)
- They call to man (Genesis 22:15)
- They carry weapons (1 Chronicles 21:30)
- They encamp around you and I (Psalm 34:7)
- They have charge (assignments assigned to you and I) (Psalm 91:11)
- They can look like a stranger (Hebrews 13:2)
- They speak to us in our dreams (Genesis 31:11)
- They excel in strength (Psalm 103:20)
- They do God's word (Psalm 103:20)
- They help us (Acts 5:19)
- They destroy (2 Samuel 24:16)
- They can touch (1 Kings 19:5, 7)
- At the end of the world, angels will separate the wicked from among the earth (Matthew 13:49)
- They bring us good news (Luke 2:10)
- They rejoice when someone comes to know Jesus as their Savior (Luke 15:10)
- They carry us to heaven (Luke 16:22)
- They are great in power and in might (2 Peter 2:11)
- They fly (Revelations 8:13)
- They warn God's people (Genesis 19:15)
- Angels go before us (Exodus 33:2)

As you can see, angels are ministers to God's people, to believers. I think one story we'll really dissect (since we are talking about warfare here) is the story of Shadrach, Meshach, and Abednego in Daniel 3. These three men wouldn't serve King Nebuchadnezzar's gods nor would they worship his idols. So they were cast into a fiery furnace as the king commanded. The Bible says the fire was seven times hotter than the usual fire. But as they were cast in this furnace, a fourth man appeared with them. The king, of course, saw the fourth man and commanded they be taken out of the furnace. The three men were not burnt even a little bit, and they didn't even smell of fire! In verse 28 of Daniel 3, it states King Nebuchadnezzar says, "Blessed be the God of Shadrach, Meshach, and Abednego who sent His angel and delivered His servants who trusted in Him."

God will send angels to "keep" us safe even in the "hottest" places we'll ever experience! It'll be really interesting to talk to these three men in heaven someday. But this story is a very real example of angels who defend us, keep us safe, and help us through trials.

It's imperative we recognize one of our weapons in warfare is the aide of angels sent from God to protect us, to aid us, and to talk with us.

You always have God on your side; He goes before you and I.

> *"Therefore understand today that the Lord your God is He who goes before you as a consuming fire." (Deuteronomy 9:3)*

He will send His angels to watch out over you, to keep you safe from harm.

I think my angels have worked a lot of overtime!

Now, this revelation doesn't give you the right to just sit down on the job! No, it actually should urge us forward to fight with more knowledge of our weapons of warfare! If not, believers will perish from the lack of knowledge (Hosea 4:6).

But with knowledge,

**"we are more than conquerors through
Him who loved us." (Romans 8:37)**

It's important to not only know your role in this spiritual war but to be aware of all the available weapons we have access to.

It is a war, but we do have the necessary equipment to conquer the battle and to come out fresh, not smelling like the fire we're in and also to be above and not below the enemy's feet.

Call upon God; ask Him to give you "all" knowledge to conquer. He'll give you what you need and so much more. I think we'll be shocked when we get to heaven and we learn how much authority we could've walked in and didn't because we just didn't know any better!

I want to walk in as much authority as I possibly can. To be a conqueror in the face of fear. To take advantage of all God gives me. And angels are our weapons of warfare, ready to aide us. Now that's exciting news!

Chapter 12

Practicing Obedience to God

"Demons Are Attached to Our Disobedience"

"We do not wrestle against flesh and blood, but against principalities, against powers, against the rulers of the darkness of this age, against spiritual hosts of wickedness in the heavenly places." (Ephesians 6:12)

We tend to forget WHO our fight is with! And then we blame God while our disobedience is actually the very reason we're struggling.

The revelation I've received is that demons are attached to our disobedience. God gives us freedom to choose. Our choices lead to either obedience or to disobedience to God.

Look at Deuteronomy 28:1:

"Now it shall come to pass, if you diligently obey the voice of the Lord your God." (Deuteronomy 28:1)

Obedience: the act or practice of obeying; submissive compliance

<u>Disobedience: refusal to comply, transgression, lack of obedience</u>

And these scriptures go on to tell us the benefits of our obedience. It says God sets us high above all nations of the earth, blessings shall come upon us, overtaking us. The heading is titled "Blessings in Obedience."

As we continue reading Deuteronomy 28, verse 15 starts with "curses for disobedience." It goes on to say that these curses shall come upon you and overtake you if you do not obey the voice of the Lord your God.

None of us like our disobedience to God to be pointed out. I think we have to recognize curses are connected to our enemy: Satan.

God covers us and protects us, but when we are disobedient to Him, we move out of that protective realm. We actually open up a door for the enemy to wreak havoc on our lives. The sad thing is, many people then blame God for the state they're in.

Nowhere in the Bible does it say God is a bad God. He brings only good to His people. He created us to walk with Him, to enjoy His love, and have dominion over the whole earth. Disobedience takes away that right. And God doesn't cause us to react as we do; we are totally responsible for our own actions.

I think it's very appropriate to link warfare to disobedience. Let me explain. Jesus died on the cross so we can live for God, eternally. Here on earth, we are subjected to the elements of the flesh. We must choose our path: obedience or disobedience. But in our disobedience, we actually are walking with the enemy. There is no middle place to live. You either live for God, or you are entertaining the enemy.

I've ran from God. I've actually lived a life of bar hopping and drinking and all that comes with that lifestyle. In my disobedience to God, I came face-to-face with the enemy of my soul. The doors

I opened were very evident. It took me many days and nights, also many hours to retrain my flesh to obey God again.

The warfare I ensued due to my disobedience was a hard lesson to learn—a school of hard knocks. But once you experience this struggle, this war, it's much easier to fight in the next round that's sure to come.

If our struggle isn't flesh and blood, why do we seem to fight against each other so much of the time? Disobedience. Disobedience is seen as anger/wrath or apathy or doubt/unbelief or self-seeking or maybe gossip. Disobedience manifests in many ways. These are only a few.

So if the enemy can get believers to turn on each other, we are giving Satan power over us. If we're fighting one another, we're probably too busy (selfishly) to see the real war: the spiritual war in the heavens. As we're fighting each other, we will not be engaged or aware of the powers of the air. Too busy with self to "see" the real war going on.

There are so many areas we are unlearned in. And disobedience is one we don't like to hear about. We've all been there at some point in our walk with God. But the warfare is highly likely to be extreme and harsh in our disobedience. The struggle is so intense we can give up and turn our backs on living for God.

I've heard many believers say when they get serious about living for God that all hell broke loose in their life. And so they backed off. They quit coming to church, not reading the Word, and isolating themselves from God's people. This is the fleshly way of dealing with warfare, not the spiritual way.

Then these actions lead to disobedience to God. No question about it, disobedience takes us down a path of making wrong choices and trying to reason it out. Because we are flesh and blood, we fight in the flesh, beating at air, therefore, nothing breaking off our life.

But as we begin to fight spiritually, things come to a head. Like a festering sore that's been oozing for a while but hasn't been dealt with yet. When we deal with the demons attached to our disobedience, it opens up a whole new can of nasty worms.

Makes me think of Jonah of the Bible. How God dealt with his disobedience. Now, maybe you won't be swallowed up by a huge fish, but all the same, God will deal with our disobedience. We try and ignore it a lot of the time, try to go about our lives as usual, but the sore is there, festering unseen to the outside. But the inside hurts without God's direction. Without the Holy Spirit's guidance, we are in a warfare fighting all by ourselves. Getting the tar beat out of us would be my guess.

I'm not trying to "spank" you here. Just pointing out it's high time believers began to live in obedience. To recognize what disobedience brings to our lives. To man up and take it on the chin. Be honest. God knows all any way. Quit blaming God for our own actions and repercussions thereof.

Let's get ourselves educated in this area of such controversy. Sin is sin. Disobedience is attached to demons. Demons are real. Warfare isn't fought with our hands but by the Spirit. We can't see the war, but it's definitely there.

Ask God to reveal any disobedience and get it cleaned up. Repentance works.

"Repent, for the kingdom of heaven is at hand." (Matthew 3:2)

Let's quit devouring one another and begin to blame the sin within for our own woes. More than likely, you're the one who causes your own troubles, not your pastor, not the church. You. Take it. Ask God to reveal this to you. He will. And then listen for His guidance.

Here are some things we need to remember:

1)   Disobedience is our own fault, no one else's!

2)   The war is not flesh. It's spiritual.

3)   Recognize who the enemy is. Satan.

4)   Don't isolate yourself from God's people.

5)   Read the Word, educate yourself/spirit man.

The fight is won by believers who are equipped. It's not always fun to hear the truth. But

> ***"you shall know the truth, and the truth shall make you free." (John 8:32)***

If this book sets even one person free, it's worth the nights of little sleep, the struggle I'm going through to get it down on paper, and the warfare I ensue as I write. It's not easy. It's rewarding, but a hard task all the same.

My prayer over you is this:

> God, hear the cry of Your people! Forgive our sins. Teach us Your ways. Give us revelation on being obedient. And may we not blame You for our own actions. Open our eyes to the truth in Your Word. Give us sharp minds that are quick to recognize the enemy and even quicker to react with wisdom from You. Teach us to fight this war in the spirit, not with our flesh. May we draw in people by our boldness. May signs and wonders follow us! Help us to be obedient at all costs. May we never turn our backs on You, the Creator and Savior of our souls. Amen.

Chapter 13

Tithing Brings Authority

"The Link to Blessings or Curses Over Our Lives"

"And do not seek what you should eat or what you should drink, nor have an anxious mind. For all these things the nations of the world seek after, and your Father knows that you need these things. But seek the kingdom of God, and all these things shall be added to you. For where your treasure is, there your heart will be also." (Luke 12:29–31, 34)

Concerning the tithe, many believers hearts' treasures are not linked to tithing. But the tithe is a law from God Himself.

"Will a man rob God? Yet you have robbed Me! But you say, "In what way have we robbed You?" In tithes and offerings." (Malachi 3:8)

Who would've ever thought I'd write a chapter on tithe in a warfare book! But as I was reading Malachi 3, it dawned on me how God's people struggle to obey the command to tithe. Then I wondered, *Why, God?* It's another spiritual fight we really don't have a true revelation of yet. But I'm hoping the Holy Spirit will give you revelation through this chapter.

Let's look at the purpose of why we tithe. In this chapter, we'll be in Malachi 3, picking away at God's Word, obtaining divine wisdom. Hold on to your seat, get comfortable with me, and let's obtain disclosure through God's Word together.

You might be thinking, *What's the big deal about tithing? What is the purpose of tithing? Why does God want us to tithe?* Glad you asked!

When God commands us to do something (as in tithing), we must react in obedience even if we don't understand "why" He tells us to.

"Bring all the tithes into the storehouse." (Malachi 3:10)

<u>Storehouse: source of abundant supplies, as of facts or knowledge</u>

It took me *years* to really get this concept. When my husband, Kevin, and I were first married, he wanted to tithe. I was not mature in the Lord and couldn't grasp why we had to tithe! Kevin was persistent, and now, forty-five years later, I am so thankful he obeyed God.

God commands us (charges us, orders us) to tithe as we can see in Malachi chapter 3.

My husband, Kevin, has a very intelligent saying when anyone tells him they can't afford to tithe. He says, "You can't afford NOT to tithe!" Just as we read in Malachi 3:9.

"You are cursed with a curse, for you have robbed Me." (Malachi 3:9)

When problems, difficulties, arise overtaking our life, normally, we can trace the reason back to our disobedience to God's commands. This is something so many believers tend to ignore and even blame God for their troubles instead of recognizing their own issues.

I could really get off on so many different topics concerning tithe, but this is a book on warfare. Maybe God will give me a book on tithe in the future!

For now, though, we will look at the warfare aspect of tithing and how we are disobedient to God concerning this issue.

Remember.

> *"The thief comes to steal, kill and destroy." (John 10:10)*

> *"And I will rebuke the devourer for your sakes, so that he will not destroy the fruit of your ground." (Malachi 3:11)*

We have to recognize and realize the enemy (thief/devourer) fights spiritually to steal from us God's promises of blessings.

> *"And try Me now in this, says the Lord of hosts, if I will not open for you the windows of heaven and pour out for you such blessing that there will not be room enough to receive it." (Malachi 3:10B)*

This chapter in Malachi is very self-explanatory. We tithe; we are blessed. We don't tithe; it opens the door for the enemy to kill, steal, and destroy the very promises out of heaven's windows!

Look at the meaning of *devourer*:

Devourer: to consume, to engulf, swallow up

Remember what verse 11 was: "I will rebuke the devourer."

So the devourer cannot consume your blessings, and he will not swallow you and engulf your life or devour your mind with fears IF we will only obey God's command to tithe.

God said He would rebuke the devourer.

<u>Rebuke: stern disapproval of, reprove, reprimand, reproof</u>

God will reprimand and rebuke the enemy for us!

<u>Reproof: censuring, rebuking</u>

In other words, God will STOP the enemy from stealing from believers if we are obedient to Him through our tithe.

In the spiritual war of tithing, we have to step out in faith. Believe God's commands are for our best. Because the devourer will take all he can and more!

We benefit greatly from obeying God through tithing. I understand (and love) to tithe now, but there was a point in my life I had no revelation of the benefits of tithing, and even more important, the curses of not obeying God through my tithe.

God's Word directs, gives us guidance, revelation, answers all our questions, and keeps us from stumbling. And in 1 Peter 5:8, God tells us to be "watchful."

> **"Be sober minded; be watchful. Your adversary, the devil, prowls around like a roaring lion, seeking whom he may devour."**
> **(1 Peter 5:8 ESV)**

When God tells me to be watchful (alert, closely observant), I am carefully paying attention to why He's directing me in this manner. To me, it's like being on the frontlines of an army; you are ready for what's coming, and you are prepared to fight the enemy. This is how God tells us to be regarding the devourer.

The opposition for a believer is in the unseen realm, region, sphere, or domain of the spirit. This is not a struggle we see with our fleshly eyes but one we have to use our spirit man to contend against—getting past our self and into the domain of faith in God.

Before I end this chapter, I want to share a vision I had while on the mission field in Mexico. Mainly the point of sharing this vision is to help you maintain a better view of the spiritual realm we can't see but is very real.

The team I was with in Mexico was a very strong prayer team. We came against a lot of darkness on this particular trip to Mexico. I couldn't sleep much as I was interceding for the Hispanic people in this city. Our group was taking ground the enemy had stolen. I had trouble resting. So I was awake in the middle of the night praying over the city and crying out to God for souls to be saved. While I was praying, I had this vision: I saw a very large soldier dressed in his Roman attire, his helmet and his coat of armor. I mean, he was seven feet tall, at least! I knew instantly he was my guardian angel. It gave me so much comfort.

What does this have to do with tithe? Everything! Our obedience in tithe opens the windows of heaven. If I wasn't obedient, I wouldn't have been on this mission trip, and I certainly wouldn't have walked in authority over the land. Blessings come as we believers obey the Lord; this includes the area of tithing.

Tithing is a link to obedience, and in turn, our obedience (especially) is a direct link to God's blessings. The enemy is well aware if you get this revelation, he loses the grip he has on your life and also on your finances and your prosperity. Don't ever think he won't steal, kill, and destroy from you. The spiritual war is a real struggle of unseen foes; your adversary is hostile and destructive toward you.

Ask God for revelation concerning tithing. He'll give you insight that'll change your life forever. And I pray this chapter has helped you understand why we are commanded by God to give our tithe.

> ***"Through God we will do valiantly. For***
> ***it is He who shall tread down our enemies."***
> ***(Psalm 60:12)***

Chapter 14

Obedience in the Warfare

<u>"Practicing Obedience to God"</u>

"For as by one man's [Adam] disobedience many were made sinners, so also by one Man's [Jesus] obedience many will be made righteous." (Romans 5:19)

"And being found in appearance as a man, He humbled Himself and became obedient to the point of death, even the death of the cross." (Philippians 2:8)

Through Jesus's obedience to God, we are made righteous. Jesus's example teaches us obedience.

Remember the meaning of obedience?

<u>Obedience: the act or practice of obeying, submissive compliance, a sphere of authority</u>

In and through our obedience to God, we obtain His authority. Obedience leads to power and authority over our enemy. If we obey His commands, walk in His ways, practice His laws, there is a sphere of authority we can walk in.

<u>Sphere: a field of something specified, to place among the heavenly spheres</u>

Look at what God says about our influence on this earth:

"Then God blessed them, and God said to them, "Be fruitful and multiply; fill the earth and subdue it, have dominion over the fish of the seas, over the birds of the air, and over every living thing that moves on the earth." (Genesis 1:28)

"God spoke: "Let us make human beings in our image, make them reflecting our nature so they can be responsible for the fish in the sea, the birds in the air, the cattle, and yes, Earth itself, and every animal that moves on the Earth." God created them god-like, reflecting God's nature. He created them male and female. God blessed them: "Prosper! Reproduce! Fill the Earth! Take Charge! Be responsible for fish in the sea, and birds in the air, for every living thing that moves on the face of Earth." (Genesis 1:26–18 MSG)

<u>Subdue: to conquer and bring into subjection, overcome, to overpower by superior force</u>

We were created by God to conquer the earth by bringing it into subjection under our God-given power. We are to overcome the enemy by our overpowering superior sphere of influence.

But to walk in that sphere of influence, we must obey God's commands to us. Obedience to God will open up an authority for us to take ground in the midst of warfare.

> ***"The Lord will establish you as a holy people to Himself, just as He has sworn to you, if you keep the commandments of the Lord your God and walk in His ways." (Deuteronomy 28:9)***

We practice basketball, football, even cooking, but we've really not quite grasped the art of practicing obedience to our Maker. And really, most of us run from obedience, ignoring God's calling of obedience to Him.

We wait until we're up to our necks in trouble before we turn to God, usually (sadly) blaming Him for the place we've gotten ourselves into.

As I consider this, I think of the Israelites (Joshua 5:6), how they went round and round in their disobedience (forty years). They were drowning in their own ignorance. God gave them commands, and they ignored His voice of reason, much like we do today. God calls us to His ways, and we choose to go our own path. Whether out of ignorance or not, it's still disobedience.

Can you imagine how much quicker the Israelites would've gotten out of their mess if they'd just obeyed? Can you just imagine how it'd be if WE would obey God's voice the first time around? And not wait until the tenth or eleventh time?

We're made to conquer, subdue, and have dominion over the whole earth. That's during warfare or during the easy-breezy times too. We must never take our eyes off God's call to obedience; the enemy will take full advantage of our lack of awareness to our surroundings.

My prayer is that through this book, you have gotten a real grasp of your spiritual state. Are you obedient during warfare? Or is it just too rough, and you tend to give up?

Remember, obedience brings power and brings God's authority into our lives.

We must practice obedience to God.

<u>Practice: repeated performance, pursuit of a perfection</u>

So in my pursuit of God's ways, I must repeatedly get into His presence. I can't sit down and give up as I pursue His voice. We only "catch" something as we strive (try hard) toward that goal.

<u>Strive: to make a strenuous effort toward any goal, to contend in opposition, to struggle vigorously</u>

I have to say truthfully that I've only made strenuous efforts or struggled vigorously for God's presence only a few times, honestly in my life. God, help us to be obedient!

Let's look at what we practice in our obedience to God.

I think the number one thing to practice is *read God's Word (sWord)*.

"Casting down arguments and every high thing that exalts itself against the knowledge of God, bringing every thought into captivity to the obedience of Christ." (2 Corinthians 10:5)

I believe the second thing to practice is *getting in God's presence*.

"And He said, "My Presence will go with you, and I will give you rest." (Exodus 33:14)

The third thing to practice is *listening for God's voice.*

> ***"Oh, that My people would listen to Me." (Psalm 31:13)***

And when we obey God, read His Word, it brings us into His divine presence which softens our hearts and opens our ears to His voice.

When we have warfare in our lives, we tend to look to God and forget His ways after the warfare has lessened. But God calls us to seek His face at all times, to keep His commands, His ways, in everything we do and say.

> ***"If My people who are called by My name will humble themselves, and pray and seek My face, and turn from their wicked ways, then I will hear from heaven, and will forgive their sin and heal their land." (2 Chronicles 7:14)***

We have vast promises from God through our obedience to His commands over our lives. Through our obedience, we can enjoy the blessings He promises us!

> Father God, shower us with Your promises as we strive to be vigorously practicing Your presence in our lives. May we be conformed to Your image and get revelation of our authority here on the earth! Help us, Holy Spirit, to be obedient so we can walk in power, authority, and dominion! Amen.

Chapter 15

In the Cave

<u>"Obtaining Knowledge on the Issues of Isolation"</u>

<u>Isolation: the state of being isolated, an act
of isolating</u>

As believers, we should never be alone in the warfare. If believers "GOT" how much authority they could walk in, warfare would not be near as rough nor would it be a lonely fight.

Have you ever been in a spiritual fight and struggled, and in the end, you wonder, *Why didn't I just get someone to help me, to pray over me, or just listen to my struggles? Why did I try to do this all by myself?*

Sound familiar? Why is it we have so much pride we don't want to admit our weaknesses?

We assume way too much about what someone will say or think about us.

The warfare we are going through is not a new thing on this earth!

Just read 1 Kings 18 and 19 to see what I'm saying where Elijah had previously "conquered" the land, then you'll see in chapter 19 he is running for his life from a woman named Jezebel.

He was in a cave, wishing he was dead. He had given up. God came to him in that cave, spoke to him actually.

"What are you doing here, Elijah?" (1 Kings 19:13B)

Today, we are no different than Elijah. We are on cloud 9 one day and stuck in a cave the next, ready to give up because we've experienced a rough bout of spiritual warfare. We "cave in" to our enemy.

<u>Cave in: to fall in, collapse, to yield, surrender</u>

I'm sure all of us has been in a cave, and you can relate to the dark, damp, and very quiet atmosphere inside a cave. Seems to me, a cave is a lot like isolation.

I've been in a state of darkness in my spiritual life. I've also spent seasons in a "cave" a time or two. Whether it's running from God or just giving up, it's a "cave" I've decided and chosen to be in.

Maybe it's time believers decide to "get up!" and decide to fight our way up out of that cave. I believe each one of us has experienced a dark season in our life. But the difference we can choose for our self is to decide not to go it alone, to break out of the darkness and shed light upon the issue of isolation.

Too many believers are just never coming out of the "cave" of the dark season. The warfare is too much to handle, and they give up. They blame others (like Elijah did Jezebel) for the state they're in. But if we take a look inside ourselves, it's in our heart we find the cause of our situation.

And no one likes to be in a dark season.

<u>Dark: no light, gloomy, cheerless, hidden,
secret, silent, a dark place</u>

I think we'd all pick light over the dark. But every one of us has dealt with hard places in our lifetime. I'm not trying to paint a dismal picture, just letting you know you're not alone in this.

It's so plain and clear to me how we can get ourselves in so much more hardship just because we choose a "cave" over letting someone help us get out of that dark season we're in.

Warfare is just that. War. War never is easy. But spiritually, it becomes a whole new battle. Because our enemy watches for loopholes in our armor. He will crawl in those holes (like a worm), and he will wreak havoc to the point of dark isolation.

So how do we get ourselves out of a dark season like this? What do we do when we're at the verge of going into isolation?

First, ask for help! Share your pain with a friend who will pray with you, help you gain back ground you've lost. Find someone who has won the battle, and spend time with them.

Second, turn on your spiritual flashlight: your Word. Darkness is always expelled by the light.

Third, listen for God to give you direction. Just as he told Elijah to leave that cave, He'll direct you too. But be sure you listen and discern correctly because in a dark season, the darkness seems to cloud our ability to hear clearly.

Interestingly, did you know that if a person spends three days in total cave darkness that they will go blind? It's so familiar to isolation. And if there ever was a time for a need to react swiftly, it's certainly in the dark cave times. The longer you spend time in a dark place, the harder it is to adjust to the light. And the longer we spend in the cave, we become blinded by our enemy.

But we also know Jesus arose from the grave in three days! Victory is ours.

> **"O Death, where is your sting? O Hades,
> where is your victory?" (1 Corinthians 15:55)**

Jesus gives us life in the darkness. He is our Morning Star. He is the way out of a dark season. He is the answer. He is the reason we are alive. He is our eternal life.

One thing is sure and steadfast: we have life in Jesus.

> **"He Himself has said, "I will never leave
> you nor forsake you." (Hebrews 13:5B)**

Many things come and many things go. But Jesus is forever. He never leaves. All else can crumble around us, but He stands firm.

The Holy Spirit led me to Exodus 20; this is where Moses is interceding for the people. God just gave him the Ten Commandments. The people were afraid of God's presence. Now look with me at verse 21:

> **"So the people stood afar off, but Moses
> drew near the thick darkness where God
> was." (Exodus 20:21)**

The revelation I've gotten from this scripture is, believers are afraid of the real presence of God, but He's even in the dark place/dark season with us. God is everywhere, all the time; He never leaves us no matter what we're experiencing.

God will call us out of the cave, and He'll bring light upon the darkness. And He'll reveal things while we are in the darkness because most of us cry out all the more in the cave than we would in the light. It's the rough warfare moments that we turn to God for help and seem to forget His presence when we're having a great moment.

I guess more than anything that we need to glean from this chapter is, don't let yourself get into isolation and go into a "cave." Let God's Word give you light for the path, in warfare or in times of quiet peace. Remember He is always with you. He will never leave you nor forsake you. His promises are forever.

Don't isolate yourself to the point of blindness where the enemy will steal from you. Keep your spiritual flashlight on: God's Holy Word.

> *"For you were once darkness, but now you are light in the Lord. Walk as children of light. Therefore He says: "Awake, you who sleep, arise from the dead, and Christ will give you light." (Ephesians 5:8, 14)*

Chapter 16

Victory in the End

"Claiming Your God-Given Right to Living Victoriously"

"But thanks be to God, who gives us victory through our Lord Jesus Christ." (1 Corinthians 15:57)

Victory: a success or triumph over an enemy in battle or war, a success or superior position achieved against any opponent or difficulty

So here, before we move on, let me explain what this means to believers: You are successful and you triumph over the enemy, Satan. You will be superior to and achieve victory against Satan or any difficulty that he may bring!

Makes me want to shout and to dance a little because so much of the time, I am fighting without a victorious mindset. Instead, sometimes, I fight not really believing that I'm the victor over this warfare. But I should be fighting, knowing, claiming my victory over the enemy.

> *"For whatever is born of God overcomes the world. And this is the victory that has overcome the world—our faith. (1 John 5:4)*

My faith overcomes the world, the enemy. By my faith, the Word tells me I can move mountains.

> *"So Jesus said to them, "Because of your unbelief; for assuredly, I say to you, if you have faith as a mustard seed, you will say to this mountain, 'Move from here to there,' and it will move; and nothing will be impossible for you." (Matthew 17:20)*

Have you ever held a mustard seed in your hand? Just one seed? It's beyond tiny! And yet Jesus refers to our faith, if we have faith as one mustard seed, that's ONE seed, we can move a mountain. Then Jesus goes on to state, "Nothing will be impossible for you."

I want to direct our attention to warfare because spiritual warfare is real, and it is our position to stand in warfare victoriously with faith as a mustard seed and where nothing is impossible for us; Jesus promises us this!

Our position, I would like to study, is the position of the blood of the Lamb and the word of our testimony.

> <u>Testimony: evidence in support of a fact, proof, open declaration or profession,</u> <u>as of</u> <u>faith</u>

> *"Then I heard a loud voice saying in heaven, "Now salvation, and strength, and the kingdom of our God, and the power of His Christ have come, for the accuser of our*

> *brethren, who accused them before our God day and night, has been cast down. And they overcame him by the blood of the Lamb and the word of their testimony, and they did not love their lives to the death." (Revelation 12:10–11)*

> *"And looking at Jesus as He walked, he said "Behold the Lamb of God!" (John 1:36)*

> *"But with the precious blood of Christ, as of a lamb without blemish and without spot." (1 Peter 1:19)*

Have you ever shared your testimony with a group of people and found out afterward that it touched so many lives? Or have you ever shared with maybe just one person and that person was shocked, that it was so relevant to their own hurts and pains? Yes. And of course, yes. We all have shared our testimony and found out after we did that there was victory because we shared our story. This is the same victory Revelation 12:10–11 talks about; we overcome by our testimony.

One of my testimonies is of "thoughts" of suicide, and every time I share my testimony, it reaches into people's hearts and sets someone free. That's the testimony that God has me share because He knows that not only I but whoever hears my testimony will be set free of the bondage of suicidal thoughts.

When Jesus died on the cross of Calvary, His blood gave us victory. That is the ultimate sacrifice for you and I to live for Him. We are justified by His act of obedience (to die for sinners like you and I.) It is in this act of sacrifice we receive victory over the enemy.

In the end of the world, God will return for believers, and we will be with Him for eternity, but until then, let's live overcoming the enemy in victory! I am tired of hearing about believers losing the battle to depression, suicide, drugs, alcohol, pornography, and many other things that bind us here on this earth!

I am ready to announce to the world, "You can win!" Because Jesus died for our sins! He gave all He had and because He did, we received all He gave.

As a mother, I can relate with giving all I have. I did it for my girls when they were growing up. This is just a tiny example of giving compared to what Jesus did for us. It's through His giving that we are victorious. The problem with most believers when we read, "Faith as a mustard seed can move a mountain," we really don't have even that small amount of faith.

> Father God, forgive us, heal our hearts and make us more like you! Because until we are like you, we won't live victoriously here on the earth! Help us to really get a revelation of who we are because of what you gave! May we have faith the size of a mustard seed! May we look at our mountains in life and demand they leave! May we never doubt your ways and your promises!

If you feel like you need to repent of faithlessness, like I just did in this prayer, take the time here and stop and talk to God. It's through our repentance God will be able to work with that mustard seed of faith and move mountains. He is willing to use you and I, even in our lack of faith! He uses me all the time in the midst of my wavering faith.

<u>"Losing Ourselves"</u>

"And they did not love their lives to the death." (Revelation 12:11B)

"I have been crucified with Christ; it is no longer I who live, but Christ lives in me; and the life which I now live in the flesh I live by faith in the Son of God, who loved me and gave Himself for me." (Galatians 2:20)

So when I live for Christ, this is really living. This is the ultimate life here on the earth! Because of Christ's sacrifice on the cross, I am no longer my own; now, I belong to God.

We really need to lose ourselves in Him. By this, I mean, we need to stop being so selfish, thinking only of our own needs or hurts, and begin to see others ahead of ourselves. If we die to our self, then we gain life in Him.

There have been numerous times I've told God, "I will get out of the way, God, so You can work through me." But there have been numerous other times that I stayed and got in the way of what God really wanted to do. See? If you have ever given your testimony, spoke for God, or just witnessed to a stranger, you will know what I mean by "lose yourself."

For an example, one time in church, I was thinking about myself, where I would eat after church, what I would say to my church friends, etc. And God reminded me by saying to me, *It's not all about you, Jen.* Wow. Okay, so God woke me up that morning! I started examining myself, really looking into my core, my heart. If we stop and really look at our heart, the issues we are having are there. I stopped that day and repented of being so selfish and self-centered.

When we die to ourselves, I mean really give it all to God:

"For to me, to live is Christ, and to die is gain." (Philippians 1:21)

On this earth, what else do we gain except Christ? We gain nothing living for ourselves, but everything is gained by living for Him. Warfare is just another area we have to realize it's not about us! The enemy comes to steal from us, and he will steal all if we don't recognize what's up.

So we have to lose ourselves to be able to battle the war of the spiritual here on the earth. We can so get in the way and cause a lot of pain and heartache in the area of warfare if we think it's all about us.

When we can stop warring among ourselves and get the revelation it's not about us or about what church you attend…it's not about you! Then your life begins to align with God's plan. That's where we begin to really live, and we die to ourselves. Dying to live for God is the best way to live!

<u>"The Believer's Superior Position"</u>

Remember what the end of Matthew 17:20 said? "Nothing will be impossible for you."

So this scripture is telling me that all things are possible in Christ, right? If all things are possible, then I am more than a conqueror through Him who loves me, right? I can win this warfare going on in the heavens. I can. I can do this!

Look at the meaning of superior and position with me.

<u>Superior: higher in rank, importance, above the average in excellence, higher in position</u>

<u>Position: a place occupied or to be occupied, status or standing, mental attitude</u>

For believers, we can and have the God-given ability to have the position of being superior. You are positioned by God to be higher in rank than the enemy. You are important to God, above the average in excellence, because you are made in God's very image. The place you are to occupy is the earth, especially with the mind, the mental attitude. Because if we win in our minds, we will win in every situation we face. Am I not correct?

As we begin to "think" we are called by God to be superior here on the earth, this then begins to align us with what God has called us to. Look at the story of Daniel in Daniel 6. I will paraphrase for you: The king made a decree that all would pray to his gods instead of Daniel's God. When Daniel heard of this decree, what did he do? He went to his house, in the window of his house, and prayed to God, just like he did every day. Daniel knew who he was in God. Daniel also would not serve any other gods. You most likely know what happens here; God saved Daniel from the lions. After seeing this miracle, the king changed his mind and let the people serve our God after he had seen how God had delivered Daniel.

Do you think Daniel even considered serving the gods of the king? No! He had a superior position, put there by God to do God's will. If Daniel would have served the gods of the king, our God would never have been able to show Himself in the miracle of shutting the lions' mouths.

The same is for us this day; we must walk in our superior position God has called us to. We have to testify with our life to the world. We have to walk worthy of our call from God. God has called each of us to walk in a position of victory. We are victors through Christ's blood shed on the cross.

Warfare is won first in our thoughts because if I think I win, guess what? I will win! But if I think I've lost before I even try, guess what? I will lose.

Our walk on this earth is all about the position we take. If I take a position of giving in to the hurts and pains, I will walk in offenses. If I take the position that God can work all things out for my good, then I will walk in victory.

It begins with our thoughts, and then we will carry out in action what we believe in our heart. Do you believe you can walk victorious? Do you believe that God has called you to walk in a superior position?

Jennifer, you say, show me that God calls me to a superior position, and I might just do it! Okay, here we go.

When you accepted Christ as your personal Savior, He is now living in you! That's a superior position. When Christ lives in you, He abides in you. That's superior. Let's look at scripture to back this up:

> *"And I will pray the Father, and He will give you another Helper, that He may abide with you for ever—the Spirit of truth, whom the world cannot receive, because it neither sees Him nor knows Him; but you know Him, for He dwells with you and will be in you."*
> *(John 14:16–17)*

Exciting news, God dwells in you! In every believer! You know God, the Helper, and you know Jesus Christ. He, therefore, dwells within your spirit! Yes!

Look at another eye-opener:

> *"Do you not know that you are the temple of God and that the Spirit of God dwells in you?" (1 Corinthians 3:16)*

Dwells: to live or stay as a permanent residence

Your body is a permanent place of dwelling that when you asked Jesus in your heart, God lives inside your spirit. You are a temple for God to dwell in. You are superior because God is in you. See?

I pray and hope this gives you some revelation as to just how important you are to God. So important that He lives in you and dwells as a permanent resident within your body, His temple.

<u>Temple: place dedicated to, any place in
which God dwells, as the body of a Christian</u>

Your body is a dedicated place for God to dwell. When God created you, He had all intentions of residing in your body, in your spirit man. This makes you a temple for God to dwell in. The blood of Jesus justifies and makes you clean, and when we are in a repentant state, we welcome God to dwell within us and to help us live for Him.

In our superior position, we can do all through Christ. Because Christ in us makes us strong. Look at what God says again referring to spiritual warfare:

"I can do all things through Christ who strengthens me." (Philippians 4:13)

In taking on our superior position as a temple of God, where God dwells inside our spirit man, we can overcome, win against Satan, and be victorious. We have to recognize who we are in Him and then follow up with our thinking and our actions in this earth. We are more than conquerors with God, and God isn't going anywhere! He is for us, not against us. He has created us to be the head and not the tail and to live above and not beneath.

The sooner we start taking our God-given position, the sooner we become what God has intended for us to be from the beginning. God created us in His image and gave us human flesh;

that flesh has choices. My choice today is to walk in my superior position. To win this battle against spiritual wars. I am walking around with God inside me! That should be adequate enough to win every battle I face!

What position are you taking? Where is your thinking taking you?

Remember, God made us to be the head and not the tail.

> *"And the Lord will make you the head and not the tail; you shall be above only, and not be beneath, if you heed the commandments of the Lord your God, which I command you today, and are careful to observe them." (Deuteronomy 28:13)*

Father God, as You dwell in us with all Your glory, may we become more and more like You. You are such an awesome God to us! May we be a temple for Your Spirit to dwell within and to use to change the world. Help us to recognize exactly who we are in and through You. Help us to walk in our superior position here on the earth, Lord. Teach us with Your Word how to be totally in love with Your people and to give our testimonies with power and Your might and love. May we touch people right where they're at and change the course of the world by loving them. Give us a heart for Your commands. Give us a heart that isn't satisfied until we live for You with everything we've got. May we be temples of the Most High God! Walking on this earth with dominion and as the head and not the tail. We can walk above the war and above the trials we face! Lead us with Your Word every day! May we listen with our ears wide open to Your voice. Thank You, Lord, for Your love for us even in our sin. You love us so much You sent Your Son to die for us. That's the ultimate love. That's what we want: Your love. Live inside of us, Lord. Dwell in our spirit man and teach our flesh to die to self and to live for You! Amen.

Chapter 17

Worship Your Way Through

"Finding Joy and Strength in the Midst of Warfare"

"Do not sorrow, for the joy of the Lord is your strength." (Nehemiah 8:10B)

I want to share with you the word from the Lord I received prior to starting this chapter on worshiping our way through. Please read carefully and receive this word from God:

My child, tell the people how you can find joy in the midst of all your trials and all your sorrows. The trials will disappear the minute you begin to worship Me and begin to replace your weakness with My strength. The answer to overcoming the warfare is in worshiping Me. Worship with all your heart and all your mind and all your soul. Worship as if I were watching because I am. I am watching every move you make, and I am guiding you this day to worship. Worship Me when you feel down. Worship Me when

you are alone. Worship Me when you feel like giving up. It is in these times I will become your joy. This is the divine joy of overcoming in your warfare. Worship me with your spirit and not with your flesh. Worship Me as if it were the last thing you do for Me. Worship with everything you have and even more. You are created to worship, and joy comes upon you as you lift your voice to Me. Joy will be your strength and help you heal up all the wounds that the trials and warfare have brought upon you. You will begin to see Me as your Father, and you will relate to who I am through this kind of worship. If you question this, just worship Me. In that worship, you will receive all kinds of joy over your mind, your body, and in your spirit. Why do you think I ask you to worship? It is to overcome the enemy.

Through our warfare, our trials, and our temptations, we can have the joy of the Lord, and that same joy will give us strength to endure those times. I was curious as to what the word *strength* meant. Look with me what it means.

<u>Strength: the state of being strong; mental power, force, or vigor; power of resisting force; is a source of power or encouragement</u>

So the JOY of the Lord makes each of us strong; mentally, we have power and a force with vigor, being able to resist the enemy. The Lord is our source of power, and He will encourage us through His joy.

When I think of joy, I think of worshipping Him. I am a worshiper. I love to worship my King. And we know that we were all created to worship the One who formed us to be worshippers. Look at the meaning of *worship*:

<u>Worship: reverent honor paid to God, adoring reverence</u>

Okay, now you know the meaning of worship; look at this: We are to pay honor in reverence to Him, adoring our Maker through our worship.

I think we need to be honest and ask ourselves here, Is my worship adoring God? Or do I just worship because everyone else in church does it?

Please be honest with yourself and ask God to help you in this area. Many people do not get the whole picture, and that's just one reason people are so bound up in trials and tribulations. We are not honoring God as He has called us to. This is an area many get caught up in the world's view. The world says it's okay to worship a man, flesh, but it's not okay to worship the Creator of our souls and the One who gave His all for us.

Many believers are walking around being beat up by the enemy because we are meant to worship God, and in turn, we receive His joy, which is His strength. He gives to us freely, and yet we let pride get in the way of giving back through our worship. Pride can cripple many areas in your spiritual life, but just remember, the joy of the Lord is our strength. So in this chapter, we are talking about pride taking away our strength. If I don't worship God, I do not receive the joy of the Lord in my life, and that takes away from me and creates weakness.

Let's look at a scripture where a man named David danced before the Lord. It is this example we need to really study and ask, Why aren't we dancing undignified like David?

In 2 Samuel chapter 6, this scripture describes David bringing the ark of God into Jerusalem. They played music while they brought the ark into Jerusalem. Verse 5 describes all kinds of instruments like fir wood, harps, stringed instruments, tambourines, sistrums, and cymbals. This was a shindig!

Then as we read on in chapter 6 of 2 Samuel, in verse 14 it states, "Then David danced before the Lord with all his might."

With ALL his might! Have you ever worshipped the Lord with all you have? With every fiber of your flesh body worshipping the Savior of our souls? Have you ever just forgotten those around you and stepped into the spiritual realm of dancing before the Lord?

Then it goes on in this chapter telling us how David felt:

> *"And I will be even more undignified than this, and will be humble in my own sight." (2 Samuel 6:22)*

At this point, David could have cared less what anyone thought about him. Because David knew what he was supposed to do: worship God. David gave thanks to God in a way that is foreign to many believers. Since the word *dignified* means marked by dignity or manner, stately, dignified conduct, I think we know how David felt about what someone thought.

It is time we believers get undignified in the area of worshipping our Savior. If God gives us strength through worship, we need to glean from worship all we can. We need to set up and recognize the world will worship just the opposite, at a cost. We need to be so undignified and on fire for God that no one ever questions who we are in Him.

We are just too prideful to "show" our ALL for God. That's the bottom line really. Let's pray to God and ask His forgiveness and start today being undignified worshippers!

Another aspect of worship I'd like to cover is the worship of shouting to God. Yes, it's in the Bible. Just read Psalms. There was a lot of shouting joyfully to God. We need to bring this worship back into our lives, our churches and worship Him just like we would yell at a football game.

Look at this scripture with me:

> ***"Shout joyfully to the Lord, all the earth;***
> ***Break forth in song, rejoice, and sing praises.***
> ***Sing to the Lord with the harp, with the harp***
> ***and the sound of a psalm, with trumpets and***
> ***the sound of a horn; Shout joyfully before the***
> ***Lord, the King." (Psalm 98:4–6)***

Okay, so what does it mean to shout to the Lord? Look at the meaning with me.

<u>Shout: to call or cry out loudly and vigorously, to speak or laugh noisily or unrestrainedly, to yell, a sudden loud outburst as of laughter</u>

Can you just picture this person in Psalms and how they must be so full of joy that it just doesn't matter what anyone else is doing or what anyone else is thinking of them. How nice to just worship God with everything and not care!

Did you know that the word *joy* is found in the Bible 244 times? I do believe God is trying to really get our attention about joy and our strength through worshipping in joy to Him. Let's not miss this. I want you to get this revelation: our warfare can be overcome through worship!

Maybe you are saying, Well, I go to a church that just doesn't worship that way. That's okay. You can start worshipping God right in the confines of your own home. Your heart can be undignified all by yourself. You will begin to be strengthened enough that you'll worship how God calls you to no matter what everyone else is doing.

If God is willing to give me strength through my worshipping Him, I'm game! I think it's vital to recognize why God states the joy of the Lord is our strength. I do believe He wants us to be strong. Don't you?

It's really high time we began to react (while going through warfare) with God's Word! React like Joshua.

> ***"Have I not commanded you? Be strong and of good courage; do not be afraid, nor be dismayed, for the Lord your God is with you wherever you go." (Joshua 1:9)***

God wants us to be strong, of good courage, and never afraid or dismayed. But so much of the time, we are all of the above! When warfare comes, we tend to back up instead of marching right into the enemy's camp and taking ground back. You know, it's human nature to *think* about things and then react slower than we should. It's our flesh though, not our spirit man who reacts in this way.

When our spirit man reacts with God's Word, this is when we begin to react with strength, courage, and no fear! Look at what God tells us in His word:

> ***"For God has not given us a spirit of fear, but of power and of love and of a sound mind." (2 Timothy 1:7)***

As believers, we can conquer without fearing; we are given by God the spirit of power, love, and a sound mind. This makes me want to worship Him undignified! With great might and with a shout or two! How about you?

The joy of the Lord is your strength, and we have access to joy, even in the warfare times. I think ESPECIALLY in the warfare! What better way to make the fear go away than worshipping God? And it will bring you strength to conquer the enemy.

I've talked about conquering in other chapters of this book; it's so real to be able to conquer with God's Word at work in our lives. It's real also to be defeated by the enemy through warfare if we don't know any better. We are unaware really of the work the enemy does, and therefore, he keeps the upper hand. Our own ignorance of warfare allows the enemy to beat us even though God has already sent His Son which allows us to conquer the earth. We are given dominion of the earth through God.

<u>Dominion: the power or right of govern-
ing and controlling, to rule</u>

I believe I've touched on dominion in a previous chapter, but it's always good to retouch on dominion because many believers are just plain ignorant in their God-given dominion here on the earth. Look at this scripture:

> ***"You have made him to have dominion
over the works of Your hands; You have put
all things under his feet." (Psalm 8:6)***

> ***"Then God said, "Let Us make man in
Our image, according to Our likeness; let
them have dominion over." (Genesis 1:26)***

God continues to list all the things we have dominion, power, and right to control and rule over: fish of the sea, birds of the air, cattle. But what sticks out to me in this chapter is this: OVER ALL THE EARTH.

Do you understand what kind of dominion you walk in when you walk with God? You have the power, the right of control to rule over ALL the EARTH! We, as believers, do not walk near to our God-given ability in the area of dominion, do we?

I know, as a believer, I do not walk in this kind of dominion. There have been a few times I've walked in dominion over certain areas of my life but over ALL the EARTH? No. BUT, I do believe God is revealing to believers all over the earth to begin a dominion walk with His power and might.

In warfare, we walk weak and afraid most of the time. But of what? An enemy that has been defeated already? Or an enemy that Jesus's blood conquered? Or an enemy who uses scare tactics and manipulation? He's a slimy worm who knows he's defeated and fights dirty. Because that's all he has.

NEWS FLASH! You have dominion over Satan! Therefore, anything he brings your way, you can fight and win. You are an overcomer and a conqueror. You are God's princes and princesses. You are His chosen people. Put on your robe of righteousness and fight with your armor. It's high time we began to ACT like royalty instead of paupers.

Look what promise God gives you and I:

> ***"But you are a chosen generation, a royal priesthood, a holy nation, His own special people, that you may proclaim the praises of Him who called you out of darkness into His marvelous light." (1 Peter 2:9)***

We are no longer "in the dark;" we know what's going on. If you've read this book, then hopefully, you know more than you did before you started. You are aware more about warfare now. Right? I hope so. That's God's plan.

The only way we are able to "proclaim" praises to God is by walking in His marvelous light. In the darkness of who we were before we came to know Him, we were blinded by the enemy. BUT now, you are walking in the light—full of knowledge of His ways and His plan for your life. You are chosen, royal, holy, and special to God. Do you think He'd call you all the above to leave at the mercy of Satan? No. He will not and has not. You are called to walk in dominion over ALL the earth.

Here again, if this weirds you out or you think it is "out there," talk to God; He will give you revelation. He will show you through His Word, through another book on warfare, or just in prayer to Him. He'll meet you right where you are. He always has, and He always will. That's because He loves you too much to leave you ignorant of warfare.

Warfare is so real, and it takes God's revelation to kick-start you into applying His Word over Satan. It's my prayer that you get so much revelation about warfare that you walk in dominion like never before and that you beat up the imps that tell you lies about our Savior.

Win or lose. What's your choice? I choose to win. Maybe I have to fight; maybe I fight daily, but I still chose to win. Maybe I get knocked down a few times, but I have been chosen to win. *Giving up* is not in my vocabulary. I will never allow a giving up or giving in to Satan's spirit to overtake me. Hopefully, this book has encouraged you to take on your God-given rights to win. You will never be the same. You Jesus freak!

All laughing aside, choose today to win. Choose to begin to walk the way God promises us we can walk: with dominion over ALL the earth. Who wouldn't want that?

> ***"Therefore we also, since we are sur-***
> ***rounded by so great a cloud of witnesses, let***

us lay aside every weight, and the sin which so easily ensnares us, and let us run with endurance the race that is set before us, looking unto Jesus, the author and finisher of our faith, who for the joy that was set before Him endured the cross, despising the shame, and has sat down at the right hand of the throne of God." (Hebrews 12:1–2)

Run in such a way that you lay aside anything that keeps you weighed down; get rid of the sin that ensnares you, and run with endurance the race that every believer must run here on this earth. Look to Jesus; He's got all the answers. Be it warfare or anything else going on, He's got the answer. And above all, dance undignified before our God!

Chapter 18

The Soul and Warfare

"Our Feelings versus Our Soul"

Have you ever said, I've got a feeling, or I've got an intuition? This is speaking in the flesh, not the spiritual. But the opposite of our feelings is in the spiritual. Through the Holy Spirit, I pray for you to receive discernment and foreknowledge and wisdom in God. Over myself, I pray this daily.

Soul: the emotional part of human nature, the seat of the feelings

So my soul is my human nature, but it also is my spirit nature. I'll explain it like this: God created us in a human body with a soul. When we accept Him into our heart, He resides in every part of our body and in our soul. Our spirit-man lives within each one of us. If we do not know God, the soul is not transformed in God. But when we know God, we are transformed by Jesus's blood, and our souls are saved from hell. When we die, our spirit beings will live with God eternally.

But if you don't know God, you will live in hell eternally with Satan. No middle ground here. Bottom line, you'll live forever either in heaven or in hell.

Nevertheless, this book is on warfare. And God started speaking to me about my soul and warfare. I was struggling with this. I mean, do people go to hell and still have warfare? I know we do not have any warfare in heaven because we will live in God's presence.

I just began typing believing God would give me answers to my questions about the soul and warfare. I thought about what Job went through. Look with me at what Job states about his soul during his hardships:

"My soul loathes my life." (Job 10:1)

"How long will you torment my soul, and break me in pieces with words?" (Job 19:2)

If you've read the story of Job, then you will understand that he lost everything: his family, livestock…everything. Satan took it all from him. This is the torment he speaks about in the above scriptures. As deeply as Job was hurting, he never turned his back on believing that God would soon give him relief. God did deliver Job. But Job stood through much tribulation.

Our soul makes room for the enemy, or God resides in our soul. No in between. We either live for God or for the enemy of our souls. Look what the scriptures say about our soul:

"He restores my soul." (Psalm 23:3)

"For great is Your name forevermore. And You have delivered my soul from the depths of Sheol." (Psalm 86:13)

God restores and delivers our souls from hell.

"You shall love the Lord your God with all your heart, with all your soul, and with all your strength." (Deuteronomy 6:5)

God calls us to love him with our all: our heart, our soul, and all of our strength. If God calls our souls to live for him, then our souls will also have warfare to deal with. If our souls can be persecuted by the devil (like Job was), then this tells me our souls will have warfare.

Makes sense because our souls are our being. The soul is our spiritual man and lives in our human body. All in one, one in all. I think of the scripture where God tells us He abides in us (1 John 4:15–16). Do you think He abides just in our spirit man? No. He abides in all of our being—our heart and our soul.

Satan will also try and reside in our soul. Since the soul is our feelings and our emotions, it makes sense that we fight an unseen warfare (but so real) with our feelings/emotions. When in all reality, God calls us to fight with our spirit man. Our souls are His; therefore, we should fight with our souls.

How do I fight with my emotions and my feelings, aka my soul? Easy. With the Word of God flowing out of our hearts and then out of our mouth. See? We fight with the Word, our sWord. I cannot stress enough how much we need to have the Word within our heart and our soul! Because since God is filling our souls, guess what? His presence then will be in our emotions and our feelings. Therefore, we cannot be "tricked" by the enemy! Because the enemy will, and does, come against our soul.

I think the answer to my question above, Will people be in warfare in hell? I looked at the meaning of warfare (keeping in mind it is spiritual). The meaning is "a conflict, especially when vicious and unrelenting." So I came to the conclusion that it's not warfare; it's torment. Hell will be full of torment and everlasting fire.

In the here and now, on this earth, we can win the warfare of the enemy. But when our soul dies, if you go to hell, it's torment—pure unrelenting torment where you will be separated from God eternally.

If you don't know God, right now, let's stop and pray this prayer together:

> Father God, lover of my soul, forgive my sins and cleanse me from all unrighteousness. May I live for You all the days of my life. Fill my soul, my heart—everything about me! Forgive me for any sin that I was unaware of too. Forgive me for any sin that separated me from You. I am Yours now! I choose to live for You forever. I choose to be your servant. Use me to bring others to You and to tell others about Your love. I choose You today. I am a new person in Jesus Christ! Amen.

If you just said the sinner's prayer, then this scripture applies to you:

> ***"There is joy in the presence of the angels of God over one sinner who repents." (Luke 15:10)***

Praise God! Welcome to the family of God!

Now, all this will make so much more sense to you, and God will reveal Himself to you in many ways.

"No Room for Fear"

As I was praying over this book, the Lord urged me to read Deuteronomy 20. As I opened my Bible to this scripture, the heading put excitement in me: "Principles Governing Warfare." I excitedly told God, Thank You, Father! and continued to read this chapter. Look with me at verse 1:

> ***"When you go out to battle against your enemies, and see horses and chariots and people more numerous than you, do not be afraid of them: for the Lord your God is with you, who brought you up from the land of Egypt."***
> ***(Deuteronomy 20:1)***

I think the biggest thing for us to "catch" here is to NEVER BE AFRAID of what we "see" in the flesh because our God is fighting the spiritual battle for us, not the flesh we see with our own eyes. But He is fighting in the spiritual, which we know is going on within our spirit man.

As we read on in Deuteronomy 20, we see the priest goes to talk with the people. Look at what he says to them:

> ***"Hear, O Israel: Today you are on the verge of battle with your enemies. Do not let your heart faint, do not be afraid, and do not tremble or be terrified because of them; for the Lord your God is He who goes with you to fight for you against your enemies, to save you." (Deuteronomy 20:3)***

It's vitally important to recognize and to catch what God is saying to each of us: Don't be afraid of Satan. Don't tremble or be terrified because of him. The Lord our God is with us in the battle against Satan to save us.

Deuteronomy 20 is very explicit and shows us that in the battle we must kill the enemies. We must battle without fear, knowing that God is with us, and He intends for us to win! He is still in the saving business!

If you continue to read Deuteronomy 20, you will see that God promises us we shall take the enemy's camp, and He also promises us "the Lord your God gives you as an inheritance." God is so into us! He wants us to know and to recognize the enemy, but more than that, He wants us to recognize that we win!

There are numerous scriptures to back up the promises God has for us. But we have to move in faith toward the goal set before us. If we are walking in fear and trembling before the enemy, then we certainly aren't walking in faith and will not have a "winner's attitude."

I think as we read in Deuteronomy 20, we can also see how God removed the "coward" from the army. He did this because the coward's fear tainted the faith of the ones who believed they were going to win. This was to protect the morale of the other soldiers. After they weeded out the cowards, then they were able to pick captains of the army to go into battle.

I want to be a captain! I don't know about you, but God did not make me to be fearful or tremble in the sight of my enemy: Satan. Rather, I am made in God's image to fight with a soul full of God's Word and fight to win. I am made to conquer the enemy, not tremble in fear and be stopped by my own "thoughts" of fear. Fear stops every spiritual move you should be making. It will keep you from your destiny, and it will also "blind" you to thinking you are already beat.

<u>Captain: a military leader, in authority, a</u>
<u>person of great power and influence</u>

God has chosen us to be leaders in His great army, to be the head and not the tail, to walk in authority over the enemy and to do this with great power and influence! He has called us to be winners, not losers. If you feel like a loser, it's time to get into God's Word and begin seeing who He says you are: a conqueror. It is possible! It's so possible the enemy tries to deceive you, and many will be deceived by his tricks and schemes.

"Ending Strong
Putting Our Weapons to Use!"

I want to look at another portion of Scripture here. I am praying you *catch* what God is showing us:

> *"And that about wraps it up. God is strong, and He wants you strong. So take everything the Master has set out for you, well-made weapons of the best materials. And put them to use so you will be able to stand up to everything the Devil throws your way. This is no afternoon athletic contest that we'll walk away from and forget about in a couple of hours. This is for keeps, a life-or-death fight to the finish against the Devil and all his angels." (Ephesians 6:10–12 MSG)*

Some highlights I want to point out: God wants you STRONG! If we go into battle weak (cowards), we will not win the battle. But if we are strong in Him, we will win every stink'n time! See?

God gives us "well-made weapons" to fight with. That's His Word, in power and in might! We wield the sWord, God's Word!

That's the ultimate weapon in any spiritual fight we face. No question about it!

With our Word, we will be able to stand against ALL (everything) the devil tries to persuade us with. It's a fight, but we can stand with the Word as our weapon!

I believe God is telling us: Don't think the fight is going to be easy; on the contrary, it will be a life-and-death fight to the finish. This scripture tells us every day we will have a fight on our hands spiritually. As long as we are living for our Savior, we will be fighting the devil.

Let's continue reading this scripture.

> *"Be prepared. You're up against far more than you can handle on your own. Take all the help you can get, every weapon God has issued, so that when it's all over but the shouting you'll still be on your feet. Truth, righteousness, peace, faith, and salvation are more than words. Learn how to apply them. You'll need them throughout your life. God's Word is an indispensable weapon. In the same way, prayer is essential in this ongoing warfare. Pray hard and long. Pray for your brothers and sisters. Keep your eyes open. Keep each other's spirits up so that no one falls behind or drops out." (Ephesians 6:13–18 MSG)*

Let's break this down together. BE PREPARED! Don't be caught unprepared or unaware of the battle. Use every weapon God is giving you! This will enable us to stand in the warfare! Apply truth, righteousness, peace, faith, and salvation throughout your life! You'll need them! God's Word will never go out void (Isaiah 55:11); it will always make a difference in every situation we face!

PRAYER. God has called each believer to prayer. In warfare, it is essential; it is life and death. Pray without ceasing. Prayer will keep you prepared by keeping your eyes open to the warfare. Be aware of your enemy, Satan. He will attack you from behind and try to take you out of the fight. He isn't playing around, and neither should we be playing. Kind of like playing with fire, you will eventually get burnt!

Lastly, this scripture says to KEEP EACH OTHER'S SPIRITS UP. Why? So that no one in the army of God falls behind or drops out. My heart literally aches at all the believers who have fallen behind in the ARMY or who have just dropped out completely.

My husband, Kevin, and I just watched a movie about a man who was a POW (prisoner of war). It was utterly astounding what all this man went through. But the other prisoners were always there for him. When he got weak, they picked him up. They would give him food. They helped him when he was in need. This is what we, as believers, should always do when we see another believer falling behind the army. We should never judge or ridicule them, never just leave them behind, never *gossip* about what they are doing and never forget them.

There are many, many believers who have dropped out because the fight was too much to handle, or they believed the schemes of the enemy. Many are "hurt" from churches treating them wrongly. Many are deceived that they are okay and do not need to be fighting the good fight of faith. Many are just in denial that God would even use them to fight in warfare.

But just like this POW, we have to step up and help others, to lift them out of their problems. To spend time getting to know what hurt them. To be their friend instead of their enemy. We are Christians—Christlike. That's what the church needs to get back to practicing. Being Christlike.

My heart weighs so heavy over the church and believers. God resides in our souls and longs for us to be His army. But without love being the center, many believers are dropping out of the great army of God. And believers must love one another to bring the lost to God.

The very center, the core of our being, our soul is full of "feelings" and full of "ideas." God created us. He created us with a soul. He also created us to be fighters. To be winners. When we begin to fight with our spirit man and not just our feelings, we begin to win the battle that rages in the spiritual realm.

Winning is the only option for me. I'm not sure where you stand in the war on Satan, but hopefully, after reading this book, from the inspiration of God, you can clearly understand your position as the believer in this army.

Do I ever feel like giving up? Of course! But do I drop out of the army? No! I don't give myself that option. I am called to be in God's great army, and I will serve my God in whatever He wants me to. Warfare is just a part of living on the earth.

Separate your feelings from your spirit man and fight this spiritual war with your spirit, living full of God's Word, with power and with might, ready and prepared to attack the enemy, even carrying one another through if we have to. Live for the destiny God has for you. Don't ever give up. Don't ever allow yourself to be cowardly or fear an enemy that is already beaten.

The very best way to end this chapter is showing you scripture. I pray as you read this you will get God's revelation!

<u>Endurance: quality of lasting—without being overcome—staying power</u>

"For God has not given us a spirit of fear, but of power and of love and of a sound mind." (2 Timothy 1:7)

"You must endure hardship as a good soldier of Jesus Christ. No one engaged in warfare entangles himself with the affairs of

this life, that he may please him who enlisted him as a soldier." (2 Timothy 2:3–4)

My prayer for you is this:

Father God, You know the hearts of each person reading this book, I pray You touch each one individually supernaturally. Fill them with power and Your love. Give them the ability to distinguish good and evil. Give them strength to endure and the wisdom to know they are WINNERS!

Thank You, kind Father, for loving us as You do. We are grateful for Your salvation and for Your Son Jesus!

Fill us with Your SUPERNATURAL POWER! Amen.

Afterword

Writing this book has been such a challenge for me. The enemy can really try and discourage! I asked a good friend of mine to pray for me, and I wanted to quote her words of encouragement: "You'll only fail if you don't do what you feel God is leading you to do. And failure is not an option with God. He's got you covered."

Thank God for good godly friends and my family who backed me all the way!

No room for failure!

And thanks to my friend Anthony for his book about the power of failure.

This helped me to finish this book with joy!

If there ever was a time for revelation in warfare, it is now. Our world is upside down and all around messed up. But as believers, we have the God-given right to fight and win the war over the darkness. We must fight with our spiritual eyes and not our fleshly eyes. We must learn what God has given us and the authority and dominion we can walk in. It is time! Come on this journey with me, and let's be the army God has called us to be! His church—together!

Jennifer Kegin, with her husband, Kevin, attends church in their community of Twin Lakes.

She loves to speak and to teach God's Word.

Jennifer has had the opportunity to travel on the mission field to Cancun Mexico, Brazil, Uganda, and Zambia Africa, Romania, and Nepal. This has been a wonderful avenue to love on God's people.

She and her husband, Kevin, live in Crescent, Oklahoma. They have three grown daughters and thirteen grandchildren, with one great-grand baby.